LONDON TRANSPORT

BUSES & COACHES

1958

LONDON TRANSPORT
BUSES & COACHES

1958

John A.S. Hambley

Published in 1999 by
JOHN A.S. HAMBLEY
7 Linden Road,
Dunstable,
Beds. LU5 4NZ

Additional text and research by David A. Ruddom

British Library Cataloguing in Publication Data
A catalogue record for this book is available from the British Library

ISBN 0 9533146 3 4

Designed by Hedgehog and produced by Hughes & Company, Kempsey, Worcestershire.
Printed and bound in Great Britain.

It is only days before the disappearance of this version of Route 86 with the first stage of the Central bus cuts implemented on 20th August following the disastrous strike. Laying over at Brentwood before departure on a short working to Romford, New Mill Inn, RT2468 clearly demonstrates the meaning of the term half-drop windows. A fast run down Brook Street will certainly ensure adequate ventilation! (M.Dryhurst)

Acknowledgements

This particular volume of London Transport Buses and Coaches 1958 contains rather more of the work of one particular photographer than usual. Fortunately he realised that although the fleet had become very standardised, it nevertheless had to be recorded for posterity. Added to the photographs found from the cameras of some other enthusiasts, it is hoped that a balanced and mixed record of the year is portrayed in the pages of this volume. For added variety a further selection of interesting pictures from earlier years that have come to light since those years were published has been incorporated. To all the photographers and collectors I extend my gratitude for allowing me the use of their photographic resources: Dave Berwick, Alan B.Cross, A.J.Douglas, Michael Dryhurst, John Gascoine, J.C.Gillham, Peter Gomm, Roy Hobbs, Roger Holmes, Fred W.Ivey, Don A. Jones, the late D.W.K.Jones, Kevin Lane, D.P.Kirker, the late Bill Legg, John Lines, the London County Council Tramways Trust, the London Trolleybus Preservation Society, P.J.Malsher, Roy Marshall, B.Montgomery, Alan Mortimer, A.G.Newman, J.G.E.Nye, the Omnibus Society, Tony R.Packer, Douglas F.Parker, Brian Pask, Photobus, the late John H.Price, Norman Rayfield, Michael Rooum, R.H.G.Simpson, John G.S.Smith, J.Thomson, Ron Wellings and Tony M.Wright. I would like to express my sincere thanks to David Ruddom for developing my rough caption drafts into the very readable contents of these books. Without his continued enthusiasm, devotion and time the books would be the poorer to the reader. My wife Iris and David's wife Enid, although not exactly filled with the love of London Transport buses and coaches that we have, nevertheless have given us great support through the long hours required to achieve this finished book; thank you both. The research for the captions has involved the use of the published work of the London Historical Research Group of the Omnibus Society, the London Omnibus Traction Society, the P.S.V.Circle and the RT/RF Register. Added information from a number of experts on the London scene, all of whom I hope are thanked in Appendix II, have greatly added to the accuracy throughout the book.

Publishers Note

I cannot emphasise enough that it is my aim to publish as far as possible 'new' work and hopefully this has been achieved in this volume. To this end I would ask that if you have prints or negatives stored away, that you might consider a loan or sale so that they may be shown in volumes still to be published. Kevin Lane prints the negatives which are lent to me and he now regularly offers his services in a number of road transport related magazines. He has built up a formidable collection of negatives over the years and offers prints at a very reasonable cost. Unfortunately the cumulated listings in fleet or route number order are no longer available at the moment. At the end of this volume however an index of all the vehicles included is given in the hope that this will prove a useful quick reference to the contents.

Introduction

In terms of the history of London Transport, 1958 will always be remembered as the year of the strike. The story of the difficult industrial relations experienced in the 1950s is well told in Ken Glazier's book 'London Buses in the 1950s' published by Capital Transport and this is not the place to repeat the tale. Needless to say industrial and political pressures resulted in an all-out strike of London Transport bus and coach operations starting on Sunday 4th May 1958 which held totally solid until 21st June when all but Bow trolleybus depot returned to work, the latter following suit the next day.

The aftermath of the strike was to continue for the rest of the year and indeed for many subsequent years. Severe cuts in services and schedules were made in August when nineteen routes were withdrawn and then a further draconian tranche of cuts followed in November. This meant that by the end of the year the operational requirement had been reduced by 546 buses and three garages had closed. These were Clapham, Putney Bridge and Old Kent Road and route numbers 4A, 7, 17, 23A, 26, 27A, 48, 50A, 58, 60, 67, 69, 127, 149, 169, 179A, 189, 238, 239, 249, 251A, 324, 328C, 346C, 351, 362A, 362B, 380, 386A, 394B, 394C, 394D, 399, 400, 407A, 415, 442, 444, 467A, 479, 492 and 804 had disappeared. Many services were amended and Saturday and Sunday operations were reduced.

During the strike the Executive allowed other operators to run services in their area. The most noticeable effect of this was overtly political since a right wing pressure group, 'The People's League for the Defence of Freedom' seized the opportunity and provided seven services using twenty vehicles in parts of London as diverse as the West End, Addington, Woolwich, Friern Barnet and Surbiton. Five more recognisable firms provided a few other services - Wrights of Harlow; Camden Coaches of Sevenoaks; Chiltern Queens; Whitefriars of Wembley and Edward Thomas in the Kingston area.

Some new routes did appear during the course of the year but in the main these were as a result of refinements of operation rather than straightforward development.

On the vehicle front the Leyland prototype Routemaster, then numbered RML3, was released by Chiswick Works and went to Willesden garage entering service from there on 22nd January on Route 8. The coach Routemaster, CRL4, was transferred in January from London Road, Romford to Reigate where, after being used to train the appropriate drivers at that garage and at High Wycombe, it plied on Route 711. Later in the year Tunbridge Wells and Windsor drivers gained training for its subsequent use on Route 704. The only other Routemaster to appear during the year was the first production vehicle RM8, which was displayed at the Commercial Motor Show.

Although no new vehicles entered service during the year many of the RTs and RTLs which had been in store since delivery in 1954 did make their appearance, giving the impression for a time at least of new vehicles unadulterated by advertisements. Two test rigs utilising RM mechanical units attached to slave bodies took to the streets shadowing buses in service to gain experience of operational conditions for what was to be London's bus of the future.

Disposals during the year amounted to 109 RTs, 134 RTLs, 13 STLs, 17 Ts, 24 TDs and for completeness, although outside the scope of this book, 14 trolleybuses. These figures include the departure of the last of the STL class which had been part of the London scene since October 1932. The first of the standard post-war RTs and RTLs were despatched to Bird's Commercial Motors at Stratford-upon-Avon in January followed by others throughout the year together with the first ones to be exported to Ceylon. In addition the first example of the Mann Egerton bodied TDs found its way to this Asian outpost in August.

Work was proceeding on converting and equipping a number of trolleybus depots for their future use as bus garages when the final (or so it was though at the time) change from electric to diesel operation got underway. That however is the story of a later year.

Traversing Aberdeen Road, Croydon on 25th October, Catford garaged RT4448 continues its journey to Selsdon, Farley Road in brilliant sunshine producing long shadows. Route 54 lost its section south of Croydon in 1973 but still runs between Woolwich and West Croydon under the same number in 1999. (Pamlin Prints)

Presumably the many passengers waiting for RT4407 to depart from Hertford bus station are familiar with the timetable of the 395/395A Hertford to Ware services. In which case they will know whether it is a 395 going to Fanshawe Crescent or a 395A to Fanham Common. The driver and conductor appear to be at odds on this point. Buses in this area have carried the familiar Fishpools advertisement for many years right down to the present day. (J.A.S. Hambley collection)

Three of the BEA 4RF4 airport coaches were transferred in June to Reigate garage, having been inactive at Shepherds Bush since receiving an overhaul in April. All sixty five of these coaches, made up of two batches delivered during the years 1952 and 1953, received their one and only overhaul during 1957 and 1958. NLP638, 639 and 640 were the three which were moved to the Surrey location, having previously always operated from the basement of Gillingham Street, Victoria garage until the wholesale move to Shepherds Bush garage in October 1957 with the opening of the West London Air Terminal. Here their passenger use is in connection with the developing Gatwick Airport. The two higher numbered of the trio, now finished in the revised livery scheme, are seen waiting outside Reigate garage in company with Leatherhead garaged RT3655. (Roy Hobbs)

With creeper now hiding much of the pebble dash on the L.C.C. commissioned council houses and a trim boundary hedge, an air or orderliness pervades Barnfield Road at Burnt Oak as RF440 waits to depart on Route 251 sometime during October. This RF had re-entered service at Muswell Hill garage after receiving an overhaul in November 1957 and is now fitted with the body first carried by RF466. (A.R.Packer)

Delivered to London Transport in April 1954, RT4746 had only commenced passenger use in March of the year now under review being garaged at Staines, having previously collected dust in the intervening years stored at Garston and Loughton garages. Just days into operation and with no advertising to degrade its highly finished exterior, it waits departure from Slough Station on a short twelve minute journey to Datchet (London Road North) by way of Route 460. Of interest is the fare stage bus stop with boarding point number 4 and the two Bristol buses with ECW bodywork parked in the background being operated by Thames Valley. (A.Mortimer)

Saunders bodied RT1816 waits departure from Vauxhall Bridge Road, Victoria for a journey on the Sunday route 57A to South Croydon Garage on 15th November. The original 57A route from this point was, with 57, the replacement in 1951 for the 8/20 circular tram route through Streatham and Tooting. However, confusion caused that 57A to be renumbered 181 in 1952. The route in this picture was introduced in December 1955 as a bifurcation of 57 on Sundays to Streatham Garage and gained its Croydon extension in May 1956. (A.R.Packer)

Ex-RT1518 saw further service with Morley's Coaches of Mildenhall in Suffolk from July 1957 until sold for scrap in 1971. A 'Grey Coaches' fleet name is carried beneath the lower deck windows. The date is 17th March and the bus is parked at Newmarket. (J.G.E.Nye)

Monday to Saturday Route 246 operating between Hornchurch Station and Harold Hill Estate had commenced on 17th October 1951 and was originally maintained by two STLs garaged at Hornchurch. RTs took over in 1954 and RT4614, carrying running plates RD92, works the route on Christmas Eve, which now runs to Noak Hill with a peak hour extension to Gidea Park. A Bedford 'CA' van has caused the bus driver difficulties in pulling in to the bus stop opposite Hornchurch Station. (A.R.Packer)

RTL482 is pictured at the 'Green Man', Leytonstone before the destination blind is changed for its next journey back to Ilford and Dagenham. The carefree approach to parking is well emphasised in this view, a far cry from today's parking problems. Body number 9065, which is currently carried, had first been fitted to a higher numbered member of the class but a further body change was still to take place before disposal in December 1966. (J.G.S.Smith collection)

TD91 is seen in Plimsoll Road, Finsbury Park on 12th July with its crew taking a rest before another journey on Route 236 to Leyton High Road, Hainault Road. The year under review was to be the last in which Leyton garage operated this type of vehicle. RF buses transferred from Sidcup took over the duties in November and this particular bus found use first at Romford and later Kingston garages before it was finally withdrawn in January 1960. Then it was included in the last but one shipment of these Leylands to Ceylon in March 1960. (A.R.Packer)

RT1016 had received an overhaul in January 1957 to re-enter service at Hemel Hempstead, having spent its previous years since November 1948 at Epping garage. It waits in Hemel Hempstead Bus Station ready for a journey to Welwyn Garden City on Route 330. The garage staff have obviously lost a 52 running plate but have shown initiative in using a 5 and a 2 instead of resorting to the chalk stick. (R.H.G.Simpson)

When delivered in 1954 a number of RT and RTL buses were placed directly into store due to the reduced requirements. In 1958 it was decided that these buses should be put into service and older members of both classes disposed of. The first of the stored buses entered service in February. RT4759, in store at Loughton garage since being delivered in April 1954, started revenue earning work at Chelsham in March. It is seen, unblemished by any form of advertising, in unfavourable weather conditions on Route 470 at West Croydon beneath the trolleybus wiring for the 630 and 654 services. A Singer car will soon overtake the bus while passengers board. (Michael Dryhurst)

Ex-RTL41 is seen on 7th April while in the ownership of J.Laurie of Hamilton, Lanarkshire who traded as 'Chieftain'. The bus later received fleet number 66 which was applied to the bodywork between the driver's cab ventilation louvres and lower window line. A repaint, rebuild of route apertures and the addition of direction indicators to the 1953 built Park Royal body belie the fact that the chassis dates from 1949. The children's play swings appear to be sturdily constructed from H section rolled metal and the bus stop shelter has been erected using corrugated sheeting, all giving an impression of Scottish utilitarian outlook. (A.J.Douglas)

Only two London garages, namely Middle Row and Stockwell, made use of RT1458 in passenger service before a one year long storage in unlicensed condition and eventual disposal in June 1956. Acquired by T.Beckett of Bucknall, Staffordshire, it was in regular service until the operator was taken over by the Potteries Motor Traction Services in March 1963. It is seen on Beckett's Hanley to Abbey Hulton service with a commendable blind display. (A.Mortimer)

RF535 was new in April 1953 as a Country Area bus but as part of the batch RF533 to RF538, had been garaged at Sidcup for around the previous twelve months prior to 1958. All received their first overhaul during the first two months of the year under review and were outshopped in Central Area colours still carrying their original bodies but having had their saloon doors removed. Except for two members they re-entered service at their former garage. RF535 however was allocated to Norbiton and is seen unloading in Cromwell Road, Kingston before turning into Kingston garage and through to the bus station. The blind is reset for its next journey to Belmont Station by way of Route 213. RF538 the other displaced bus re-entered service at Muswell Hill garage. A fine example of a MkII Standard Vanguard car is about to overtake the bus. (Michael Dryhurst)

Standing out from the gloomy weather conditions at Trafalgar Square on 16th November with the National Gallery to the right, RTL1090 lays over on Sunday only Route 44A. This Charing Cross to Mitcham service operated for the last time on 23rd November, having been introduced five years earlier on 11th October 1953. The bus completed thirteen and a half years service before being disposed of in May 1964 to the Ceylon Transport Board to continue in passenger use. (A.R.Packer)

En-route for South Wimbledon Station on Route 189, newly overhauled RTL1040 carries CA7 running plates. This route had been introduced on 7th January 1951 with the second stage of the tram conversion programme and was to survive until the August upheaval of the year under review. Its suffixed A counterpart, introduced on the same date, continued to operate, being extended to cover some of the lost route. It was renumbered plain 189 on 26th November and transferred to operation by Merton garage with the closure of the Clapham base. (F.W.Ivey)

Middle Row garaged RTL20 is in Walterton Road, Westbourne Park on 23rd March, very shortly before being withdrawn from passenger service and placed in storage at Stockwell before sale in September. It was fitted with body number 6605 of RT8/2 classification, being three years junior to the chassis on which it is mounted. (A.R.Packer)

TD36, having disgorged its passengers, stands in Cromwell Road before turning a sharp right to enter Kingston garage and run through to the bus station for another journey to Church Cobham on Route 215. Driver and young conductor complete with his Gibson ticket machine have a few words before moving from the hoardings which include enticements to see the 'most daring story ever told on the English stage' at the Chiswick Empire. (Photobus)

The Central bus seasonal services of 1958 reverted to their winter mode though with a number of variations during October and November. One casualty of these changes was the Hounslow to Highgate Sunday Route 27A, but not before RT1204 was caught by the camera as it passes the elegant Chiltern Court development of the Metropolitan Railway, built over their Baker Street Station in the late 1920s, although the style was of Edwardian opulence. (R.Wellings)

East Midland Motor Services Ltd. had gained ex-RT1456 with several other vehicles from Wass Brothers Ltd., Mansfield on 1st April of this year giving this example the fleet number D45. Having sustained roof damage it stands in an East Midland depot awaiting attention on 11th May, not quite six weeks after acquisition. Its passenger carrying career ended by 1964 becoming derelict with its last operation, Todd Luxury Coaches of Whitchurch, who were its fourth operator having acquired the bus by September 1961. (R.Holmes)

Laleham, a small quiet Thames-side village in Middlesex with reservoir and gravel pits on three sides, was served by Central Area routes 218 and 224, both of which were worked by the 1/1TD2 type of bus. In July Uxbridge garaged TD128 lays over in The Broadway before resumption of duties and a return journey to its home town. (M.Dryhurst)

Sunday only service 102A was introduced on 5th October of the year now under review to operate between Golders Green and Chingford Hatch, replacing the Sunday service on Route 191 at the eastern end. Standing in the trolleybus lay-by at Golders Green on 28th December, RT2410 carries AD53 running plates. Behind, pedestrians head along the footpath towards the tube station and main bus station. (A.R.Packer)

On Sundays Route 10 terminated at London Bridge Station leaving the section through to Victoria via Borough and Lambeth Bridge for other routes to cover in piecemeal fashion. RT1199 with T7 running plates waits departure from a rather damp London Bridge terminal to Woodford Bridge having been a resident of this north-east London garage since July 1957. Leyton garage of course will always be remembered as having the honour of putting the first post-war buses of the class into service in May 1947. Saunders bodywork is still fitted to this vehicle which carried a 7/57 overhaul date on the rear platform. (R.H.G.Simpson)

TD122, now garaged at North Street, Romford and in use on Route 250, still appears to have managed to keep much of its lustre from when last overhauled in January 1957. It is seen on 24th December with a typically heavy passenger loading while waiting to continue its semi-rural journey from Romford town centre through Havering-atte-Bower, Stapleford Abbotts, Abridge and Theydon Bois to Epping Town. The shops in the picture are typical of the retail facilities of the period before shopping malls were thought of and, as was so often the case, at least two rival shoe shops have settled very close to each other. (A.R.Packer)

The twenty five London Transport RTs acquired by Bradford Corporation during the year were pressed into service very quickly, having been repainted in the attractive Corporation blue with a single primrose relief band between decks. With the London via points box panelled over and carrying fleet number 412, ex-RT174 is seen as it traverses the Bradford city centre with two differing bodied baby Austin A30s keeping it company. Owned by London Transport from September 1947 through to March 1958, the bus moved that month to Bradford where it remained until being disposed of as scrap to Autospares, a dealer of Bingley, in May 1966. (A.D.Packer)

Carrying considerable grime, doubtless from its forays through Epping Forest to Loughton on Route 38A, RT1348 waits departure on the 8th February from busy Victoria Station forecourt. This is one of Leyton's minority allocation to the route and carries running plates T54. RT4697 on Route 134 with running plates J9 is the only other identifiable vehicle in this crowded scene. (A.R.Packer)

RT2521 with chalked running number 203 waits for further use as a 705 relief between Central London and the Biggin Hill Air Display. Normally resident at Dorking garage it has joined the variety of vehicles that will have been loaned to Dunton Green for the occasion. The advertisement 'Beer - the best long drink in the world!' is unusual in not relating to any particular brewer's product. (A.Mortimer)

GS38 is seen standing at Oxted on 20th September with running plates CM42 while waiting to return to its garage at Chelsham after duty on Route 464. This bus had initially entered service at Epping garage in December 1953, re-entering passenger use at Chelsham after its October 1956 overhaul. Upon its next visit to Aldenham in December 1960 it was returned to Dunton Green where it spent its remaining years before withdrawal in March 1965 and eventual sale to the British Railways Board (Western Region). (A.R.Packer)

RT1214 entered service at Middle Row garage in September 1949 fitted with a Saunders' body and in Central Area red livery. Here it is seen at the Uxbridge Underground Station terminal of Route 305 working from Amersham garage in Country Area green. It received this livery in September 1957 at the time of its previous overhaul when it also received this RT8/2 body. (A.Mortimer)

Park Royal bodied RT4344 is bound for Teddington Station when photographed outside Richmond Station on 27th December. Route 270 had been introduced on 2nd May 1956 to operate Monday to Saturday from Kensington, Queen's Gate to Teddington Station being a localisation of the long-standing route 27. The 270 seen here was withdrawn in February 1963 and must not be confused with a later 270 which commenced on 20th April 1970 running between Richmond and Fulwell and now numbered R70 in an extended form. (A.R.Packer)

Wednesday half-day closing in Walton on Thames and RLH14 on Route 461A passes the deserted shops in the town centre as it journeys to Botleys Park, St.Peter's Hospital. Although this particular route did not require the use of lowbridge type vehicles, they were officially allocated since it inter-worked with 461 which did require them. Throughout its entire nineteen years of service with London Transport this bus was only ever allocated to Addlestone. Subsequently it was one of many eventually shipped to the U.S.A. (M.Dryhurst)

Ex-STL2595 is seen providing recreation facilities for children along with some home built playground equipment. This STL is documented as having been in the ownership of W.C.French, contractors of Buckhurst Hill as their fleet number 975, having been acquired via W.North of Leeds in April 1953. It is known that some of the vehicles owned by this contractor were never actually used, only being purchased for their engines or other mechanical parts. Careful inspection of the bodywork suggests this is the case in this instance. On the reverse of the photograph it is stated that Brigadier Todhunter of Threshers Bush, Hunter's Hall Farm, Harlow was the custodian of this 15STL16 when the photo was taken. Did the Brigadier have W.C.French connections? (Photobus)

RTL541 is seen at the north end of the Blackwall Tunnel in Poplar in use on Route 108 to Bromley by Bow and operating out of its final London Transport garage, Athol Street, Poplar. In the distance two further RTL buses can be seen on the Robin Hood Lane stand for Route 56. In January 1961 the main subject of this picture was exported to Ceylon carrying body number 3705, with which it is seen here. (F.W.Ivey)

This close-up is of the Old Kent Road garage plate on RT1170. The premises in Bowles Road had a long career spanning the horse tram period through to the RT and RF era. After transformation into a bus garage in the Edwardian period from its previous use as a horse tram depot, many types of buses including the memorable Inter-Station C type vehicles and G436, the experimental Meadows engined Guy were operated. Coded V when its Vanguard owners were absorbed by the LGOC in 1908, it gained its P code in 1911 in a general re-coding exercise and used this code until its closure in the year under review. (A.R.Packer)

Saunders bodied RT1170 was resident at Old Kent Road garage for around sixteen months before a further transfer sent it to garages north of the river for a good number of years. It waits at Surrey Docks on 15th November before further use on Route 1 to Marylebone. In 1958 until its closure on 26th November, Old Kent Road garage provided the major allocation to the route, with Cricklewood adding seven buses on Sundays when the route still followed its traditional working north of Marylebone to Willesden. The South London garage had only had a daily allocation on the 1 since 1956. Prior to that its involvement had been a pre-war supplementary service between Bermondsey Square and Surrey Docks and a Sunday involvement since 1951. (A.R.Packer)

Now in a livery of dark green with cream central band, former RT1432 is seen at Hanley on 16th March while in the ownership of T.Beckett & Sons Ltd. of Bucknall on a route from Hanley to Bentilee via Beverley Drive and Lauder Place. PMT of Stoke on Trent acquired the Beckett business in March 1963 but this and the eight other ex-RTs involved in the acquisition were never operated by their new owner. John Dengate & Son Ltd. of Beckley made further use of the bus as their number 38 between July 1963 and May 1965 prior to it being scrapped by Hoyle, one of the dealers of Wombwell. (A.R.Packer)

RTL38 and RTL39 keep each other company at the Bird's Commercial Motors premises during March, reminiscent of their initial passenger use together at West Green garage in January 1949. When acquired by J.Laurie, trading as Chieftain, later in the month they were still inseparable, carrying fleet numbers 60 and 61 respectively. The parting eventually came in 1965 when the lower number vehicle was scrapped, having suffered accident damage. (J.Gascoine)

TD39, looking very presentable, waits departure from Norbiton garage in November of the year under review at the start of what was to be a further career with the Ceylon Transport Board. The bus had first entered service in November 1948 operating from Enfield garage, transferring to Kingston in May 1953 where it completed its passenger service years with London Transport. It was then included in the first bulk shipment of the type to Ceylon in January 1959, the type having received approval for use by the Ceylonese authorities after TD57, exported some five months earlier, had proved successful. (J.A.S.Hambley)

Seven Kings garaged RTL764 is viewed with crew parked at Stratford Broadway on 16th November before departure on a journey to Little Heath via Route 25A. With the third stage of the Central Area route alterations which commenced on 26th November, this Sunday only route would be withdrawn to be covered by an extension of the 129 to serve Little Heath. The hoarding behind the bus covers the bomb damaged remains of the old Stratford Empire, originally built in 1898 and which was finally demolished in the year under review. (A.R.Packer)

On 12th July at Finsbury Park three buses on the Route 233 stand portray the usual pattern of operation on this route between 1955 and March 1959, at which time the road under the railway bridge in Station Road, Wood Green was lowered allowing double deck operation throughout. This is a Saturday, proved by the fact that West Green's RTL1620 at the front is destined for Alexandra Palace, The Dive which was within the Palace grounds below the television mast. At other times the double deckers turned at the Victoria Hotel at the Palace gates. (A.R.Packer)

Route number 69 disappeared with the third stage of route alterations commencing November 26th although the service on a Monday to Saturday basis was unchanged, merely being renumbered 36B. This was a poor exercise in public relations since an outcry ensued from people under the impression that the service had been withdrawn completely and the road left to the existing 36. RT2655 is seen at Vauxhall Bridge Road awaiting departure for Grove Park. No.282, which is the white painted shop beyond the bus, will be remembered by older readers as the original Ian Allan premises. (A.R.Packer)

Now fitted with Saunders bodywork, RT206 stops at 'The Crown', Cricklewood on its journey to Victoria on Route 16. The public house forecourt, which was once host to horse buses and early motorbuses is now full of private cars and the buses must travel up the road to Cricklewood garage to find a suitable turning point. The body number 2576 had carried this fleet number since re-entering service after overhaul in January and after its next visit to Aldenham in February 1962 it would re-appear with fleet number RT1793. (A.R.Packer)

GS61 sits in the Great Yarmouth Corporation Transport garage one Sunday afternoon in October. Keeping it company are a Leyland TD5 with Weymann bodywork and a Guy Arab II with utility Park Royal body. Following its extended loan it returned to London in July of the following year together with the other members of the batch, having been replaced at the seaside town by six new Albion NS3N model fitted with Willowbrook bodywork for continued one-man-operation. (M.Dryhurst)

Waiting in the low angled sunshine at Chesham Broadway during December, GS34 pauses between duties on the very short 348A route to the Pond Park Estate which had a ten minute journey time. Amersham garage, in line with Chelsham and Epping, eventually succumbed to the larger RF class in October 1962, their entire complements of GSs being dispersed far and wide with a large proportion entering storage. (A.R.Packer)

RT4554 awaits departure from the Uxbridge terminus of Express Route 803 on a short working which will terminate at Garston L.T. Garage. The route blinds were white on a blue background which was the London Transport standard at the time for express services. In the background red liveried RT911 with RT3 bodywork waits departure on a journey to West Drayton Station by way of Route 223. (M.Dryhurst)

A cold and damp December day sees RF508 at Loughton Underground station with the only warmth being shown around the engine with the exterior panelling in the immediate area drying off. The route blind has been re-wound for a return journey on Route 254 to South Woodford Station, to which point the service had been extended on weekdays from Buckhurst Hill Station on 8th January. Since disposal in June 1977 for preservation, though with a different body to that shown here, the bus changed hands several times including spells of passenger service and school use but it is now once again in preservationist's hands. (A.R.Packer)

The year now under review proved to be the final year for entry into service of 'new' RTL buses, while during the same period the first of the earlier examples were disposed of. RTL1579 was in store at Garston since its delivery in September 1954 and eventually entered service in April 1958. At Victoria Station forecourt it is seen in use on Route 29 soon to depart for Southgate Station, being garaged at West Green. Further from the camera Cricklewood garaged RT2365 also takes a well earned rest from its duties on Route 16. (K.Lane)

The route number 235 was resurrected on 12th October 1955, having lain dormant since 12th May 1942 when a service between South Croydon and Selsdon operated by single deck LTs had been withdrawn. The new route was in response to local demand for a service to the Richmond Hill area which, although close to the town centre, involved a hard climb, particularly if you were laden with shopping. The single bus provided by Twickenham garage was, on this occasion, RT1339 and it stands in Friars Stile Road as the driver makes sure he is in the picture. The route survived the cutbacks in the aftermath of the 1958 strike but succumbed to the 1966 overtime ban after which it was in the hands of independent operators. (A.R.Packer)

Ex-London Transport vehicles were first added to the fleet of Samuel Ledgard in 1953, comprising a batch of fourteen Daimler buses. Former D280, with its original Park Royal body, journeys to Otley surrounded by various other road users. Austin, Hillman and Morris models are represented while a three wheeled invalid car adds further interest. The bus was finally scrapped by Holmes, a dealer of Leeds, in 1961 and the same dealer saw to the demise of ex-D226 from the same operator. (R.F.Mack)

In around four years time red liveried RT4610 of Forest Gate garage will receive its second overhaul and be outshopped from Aldenham in Country Area colours. If we look even further into the future the reverse situation took place with its October 1965 visit, clearly a bus which wanted to experience service to the full! Here on 24th July it is parked at Stratford Broadway having worked a short journey on Route 96, which was another route to be removed after 19th August. (A.R.Packer)

Standing at Edgware with the Christmas holiday just days away, RT758 awaits departure for a journey to Oxford Circus on Route 113 with running plates AE12. Having first entered service in July 1948, the bus achieved a commendable twenty two years of operation within the capital before disposal to the Wombwell Diesel Company for scrapping in November 1970. (A.R.Packer)

GS11 drops off its passengers at Oxted while in service on Route 464 on 20th September. The blind reads 'Oxted, Barrow Green Road & Holland via Pollards Oak' indicating that the bus is operating one of the journeys which worked a loop at Hurst Green to serve the Pollards Oak area to the east of the railway line. This had been introduced in May but was not implemented until 22nd June on the resumption of normal services after the long strike. (A.R.Packer)

All three seated passengers appear inquisitive as to why someone should want to photograph RT760 while waiting on the bus stand at Rennell Street, Lewisham on 15th November. Note the blank red slipboard in place beneath the canopy of the New Cross garaged bus while RT2443 parked behind carries the usual black variety announcing 'To & From Regents Park' in its use on Route 1. (A.R.Packer)

Route 489A operated between Meopham, Hook Green and Gravesend where RF659 waits with running number NF11 on 6th December. This Country Area bus had been outshopped from its Aldenham overhaul in August for one-man operation, although this offside view shows no sign of use in its new configuration. Although only recorded as receiving one further overhaul in September 1962, it actually continued in passenger service until August 1974. Disposal followed in February 1976 when it was scrapped at Wombwell Diesels, ending an existence which stretched back to its entry into service at Guildford in September 1953. (A.R.Packer)

Apart from the registration, Belfast Corporation fleet number 496 hides its previous identity of D188. The new 1955 Harkness bodywork is a great improvement on the relaxed utility style previously carried on the hundred buses delivered as D182 to D281 in 1946 to help relieve the chronic situation the Board found itself in immediately after hostilities had ceased and before the RT could get into production. The bus is seen in Belfast city centre with an alighting only bus stop in evidence while the Eirco (Wholesale) Ltd. window display of refrigerators adds some brightness to an otherwise dreary background. (D.F.Parker)

At London Bridge Station Middle Row garaged RTL1174 has attracted a scattering of passengers on 15th November for its next journey to Acton High Street carrying running plates X7. The 7A service had been extended to Acton from East Acton at the time of the August withdrawal of Route 7. (A.R.Packer)

Former RTL5, immediately following repainting into its new owner's livery, demonstrates the large amount of work and expense needed to bring the vehicle up to the high standards required by E.Emmerson, who traded as O.K.Motor Services. The livery is now a maroon colour with cream surrounds to the windows, complemented by red and cream lining out. The bus had been one of the original production models which entered service at Sidcup garage from 1st December 1948. On page 130 of the 1950 book of this series it can be seen in almost as new condition. Disposed of in February of the year now under review to Bird's of Stratford upon Avon it was immediately acquired by its Bishop Auckland operator, who added a further substantial number of years to its operational life. (A.Mortimer)

Due to the unfortunate situation of a combination of over estimating vehicle requirements and declining passenger use, the first sales of the standard post-war RT family type buses was made in January of the year under review. The lowest numbered of the RT marque to depart was RT166 and together with nine further members and six Leyland RTLs it made its way northwards to Bird's Commercial Motors. Independent operators, aware of a bargain, snapped up these vehicles. The executors of S.Turner, Brown Edge, Stoke on Trent put RT166 into service as their fleet number 8. It was to be a familiar sight in and around this area of the Potteries until withdrawn from service in January 1967 when it was consigned to the scrap heap. (Michael Dryhurst)

Route 199 was introduced on 10th October 1957 for a Monday to Saturday service between Waterloo and Farnborough. This was a part localisation of Route 1 and the choice of 199 was rather quirky. Seen here at the northern terminal on 19th August, Catford garaged RT1778 waits departure for Farnborough. RTL798, next in line, carries Route 196 details while the furthest identifiable vehicle, RT3316, displays blinds for Route 260. (A.B.Cross)

An offside view of ex-T416 appeared in the 1957 book of this series and this nearside view is included to show the various small alterations which were carried out on the exterior of the bodywork. An opening has been inserted into the canopy together with an even larger one just forward of the rear wheel arch. While the latter may be for luggage, the immediate use of the former is obscure. The corner mounted driver's mirror has been repositioned beneath the canopy while a width marker light is in place which mirrors that fitted to the offside. In this picture the vehicle is seen standing in the Green Line's depot at Point Chevalier, Auckland, New Zealand sometime during sunny October in the current year under review. (D.P.Kirker)

North Street, Romford garaged RT3540 lays over in Wangey Road, Chadwell Heath on Route 86, still needing its destination to be reset for the next trip east towards Brentwood. This is 24th July and the route was one of nineteen withdrawn completely with the first stage of the Central Area bus cuts imposed on Wednesday 20th August. The bus fared little better either for on its next visit to Aldenham for overhaul it was outshopped with a roof box body, number 2031, which guaranteed an early exit from London which occurred in February 1965. (A.R.Packer)

With a fine looking Timpsons Duple bodied AEC Regal IV of 1952 to the left of the picture, much travelled former D152 departs the Wembley complex on 26th April, now in the ownership of Margo's (Bexleyheath) Transport Ltd. showing a decidedly vintage telephone number in the route box. It had been one of only two vehicles which entered service with East Yorkshire Motor Services Ltd. when they acquired the White Bus Company of Bridlington in November 1955 who were the initial owners of the bus after sale by London Transport in March 1953. It was acquired by Margos in February of the year under review via the dealer P.D.Sleeman of London, W.5. (A.R.Packer)

New Sunday only limited stop hospital Route 400 was introduced on 22nd June although it had been due to start operation with the summer schedules of the Country Bus Department on 14th May, which were delayed by the strike. Provided in order to link the estates of New Addington with Warlingham Park Hospital, the route was not a success and was withdrawn with the winter programme having only operated on 17 occasions. GS47 inaugurated the service and it is seen at the hospital entrance on the first day. (A.G.Newman)

Holloway garaged RT573 stands beside one of the thirteen staff canteen trailers which were strategically placed around the system with this particular example providing the much needed 'cuppa' for bus crews at Plimsoll Road, Finsbury Park. The trailer is parked on what was to be the site of a purpose built canteen after 20th October in the year under review. Route 19 is a very long-standing route, dating back to London Road Car's Route H between Highbury Barn and Clapham Junction which started in 1906. The bus seen here, although by then fitted with a non-roof box body, became one of the RTs used as staff transport by Lesney Products Ltd. of London E9 after its disposal in December 1976. (A.R.Packer)

RT976 had initially entered service at Hertford in October 1948 and upon its first overhaul in June 1956 re-entered service at Epping. Seen in its home town garage yard on 13th December, it carries running plates EP203 in readiness for its next use on the Harlow Town Service 805 which, as the blind shows, worked in service to and from Epping garage. A further overhaul in May 1960 with subsequent service operating from St.Albans garage was followed by storage at Garston before disposal in May 1964 and export. (A.R.Packer)

Unfortunately the photographer did not provide details of what is going on in this picture. The bus, RT3269 in the centre of the picture, is holding up a queue of buses trying to get into the Victoria Station forecourt. It carries running plates GM10, is blinded for Route 10 but carries a Neasden (Dog Lane) destination which is appropriate to Route 16. It appears to be making for the Route 16 bay (a real Route 10 vehicle can be seen beyond). Up until 22nd November Victoria garage had a Saturday allocation of ten buses on the 16, so maybe it is just taking up service and it has been left to the conductor to sort out the number and via point blinds. (R.Wellings)

RF585 is seen in its new passenger carrying mode as a one person operated bus, having re-entered service just days earlier from an overhaul which also resulted in a body change. Its previously fitted RF2/2 example numbered 8762 was replaced by this RF5/1 version numbered 8871 which had previously been mounted on RF694. Sometime in December and with a Christmas tree in place, Chesham town readies itself for the festive period. Note that the direction indicators on the bus are tucked out of use, possibly yet to be wired up. (A.R.Packer)

RFW5 is seen in company with other representatives of the coach travel industry while parked within Victoria Coach Station. At an advantageous height 'Skyways' advertise their service to Paris for £7.19.0 which translates into £7.95 since decimalization. The arrow points to the Skyways terminal 'at far end of station', well away presumably from the BOAC's imposing building which forms the background to the hoarding. (Photobus)

On 5th July RTL62 nears the end of its passenger use within the capital, being withdrawn from service in August. In January of the following year it was exported to Ceylon and body number 4434, looking most presentable and first mounted on the chassis of RTL44 would find itself in a very different environment. RTLs were not common on Route 25 in 1958, the bulk of the route's allocation being RTs from Forest Gate. However, Clay Hall supplied a handful of these 7'6" Leylands, although their Saturday involvement was removed after 26th November. (A.R.Packer)

August 20th was the last day of operation for Route 127 which in its fairly short existence had made use of low bridge buses from the various classes operated by London Transport, although it had commenced operation on 22nd January 1941 using Manchester Corporation Transport vehicles of similar height. RLH71 had been allocated to Merton ever since its initial entry into service during December 1952. In the rest of its passenger carrying years however it would experience service from all the Central Area garages which made use of this type of bus. (J.Gascoine)

Northfleet garaged RF607 is seen at the Gravesend Clock Tower setting down point on 6th December about to move to the stand to await its next journey on Route 489 to the White Swan at Ash. Delivered as a 41 seat Country Area bus in July 1953, conversion to one-person operation with 39 seats took place in October 1957 to be followed in March by the first of its three overhauls, on this occasion retaining its original body. (A.R.Packer)

The one hundred D class buses which had been acquired some two years earlier by Belfast Corporation were fitted with new Harkness bodywork during the years 1955 and 1956. Ex-D75, seen parked in Donegal Square South, carries its new owner's coat of arms and fleet number 506. (B.Montgomery)

Deserted one man operated RF620 parked in Hertford Bus Station on 11th October waits its next journey on Route 342 to New Barnet Station. Prior to 23rd July the route had operated from Broxbourne via Hertford to New Barnet but by the time this photograph was taken it had been withdrawn east of Hertford. The choice of Brookmans Park as an intermediate point on the blind was a little misleading since, although the route served the Great North Road, anyone wanting the centre of the village would have a mile and a half walk. (A.R.Packer)

Entry into service of the 281 D class vehicles commenced in May 1944 and was completed in November 1946 with withdrawals commencing in August 1952 and ending in January 1954 when the final examples at Sutton were ousted by RTs. D84 entered service in April 1945 fitted with Duple utility bodywork seating 56 and was withdrawn in April 1953. T.Burrows & Sons of Wombwell acquired the vehicle in June of the same year via W.North and Sons, the Leeds dealer. Allocated fleet number 81 it was rebodied with a Burlingham 62 seat body in March 1958 which incorporated doors at the rear. It is seen leaving the Leeds Central Bus Station on 7th August in a red and white livery. Although Yorkshire Traction acquired the business in October 1966 none of the Burrows vehicles saw service with the new owners. This bus was scrapped in 1967 by Hibbins, a dealer of Ramsey. (A.R.Packer)

RTL85 is seen at Clapham Common on 16th November with the long-standing hosier, hatter and menswear specialist retail premises of Arthur Knock helping to pinpoint the well-patronized bus stop. Still to receive two further overhauls before completing its passenger career, the Leyland chassis was then stripped of all useful mechanical parts before the remains were disposed of to Pickersgill & Laverick, a dealer at Cudworth, 3½ miles from Barnsley in June 1969. (A.R.Packer)

This looks like crew changeover time for Upton Park's RT4699 on Route 145 at Ilford on 24th December. Returned to service after overhaul in May 1957 to Upton Park garage, the bus stayed there until December 1960 when, after a further visit to Aldenham, it re-entered service at Enfield. (A.R.Packer)

Photographed in March, RT1224 illustrates the early fitting of trafficators as it stands on the artistically laid cobbles at Golders Green station. A small number of RF and RT vehicles had been fitted with this latest aid to road safety in 1956. It proved such a success that the whole fleet was equipped once adequate supplies were available from 1959 onwards. (A.R.Packer)

About to depart from its terminus at Caterham Station, RT3816 in use on the 482 Limited Stop service to Smallfield Hospital has attracted a number of passengers, most of who have taken advantage of a seat in the upper saloon. The route had been introduced on 1st March 1953 and was operated by a Godstone garaged vehicle. Running on Thursdays and Sundays it lasted through to 1972 although the Thursday service was withdrawn in 1967. The RT had returned to service in February 1958 from its first overhaul and remained at Godstone until a further visit to Aldenham for overhaul occurred in January 1962. (J.A.S.Hambley collection)

Now operating in totally unfamiliar territory and re-registered 22-Sri-1443, ex-RT251 displays the high quality condition in which the influx of RT buses could be found when they commenced service in Ceylon. The Ceylon Transport Board had been formed on 1st January of the year under review and their emblem is carried where once 'London Transport' would have graced the panelling. Certain windows have been replaced by sliders to help combat the humid conditions found on the island. To the left of the picture an RTL is still running in as exported condition. (J.A.S.Hambley collection)

RT167 garaged at Old Kent Road passes Great Portland Street Station on the Metropolitan Line on its way to Surrey Docks Station by way of Route 1. This mid morning July scene of abundant greenery, elegant street lampposts, wide uncluttered thoroughfare and well preserved period buildings is typical of the area bordering Regents Park and which is spoilt today by the volume of traffic. (M.Dryhurst)

The destination blind has been wound for the return journey on Route 260 to Cricklewood Garage by RM1 as it stands at Waterloo bus park sometime during January. This was RM1's longest period of service, working Route 260 on weekdays and Route 2 on Sundays, but in all less than three years were spent in actual passenger service. (A.R.Packer)

Passing Hainault Forest on 4th August, RTL400 is seen on Route 139A as it nears the end of its journey from Dagenham at Chigwell Row, Maypole Inn. The route number had been introduced on 26th May 1946 for a service which ran on summer Sundays only at first but became the regular Sunday service after 1949. It last ran on 23rd November of the year under review. Interestingly the driver still sports a white summer dustcoat, even at this late date. The bus soldiered on until departing London Transport ownership for scrap in February 1970.
(J.G.S.Smith collection)

Golders Green Underground station forecourt is still surfaced with the well worn and sometimes slippery road sets in this picture taken on 28th December. In this day and age of low loading attributes of vehicles now entering service it is interesting to note the lady about to drop out of the RT on Route 183 now decanting its passengers to the left of the picture. Alperton garaged roof box RT3349 demonstrates the three line via point blinds experimentally used in the mid-nineteen fifties. Five lines of information had previously been carried including Ealing and Hanwell but these places have been omitted in an attempt to gain greater clarity. (A.R.Packer)

En-route for Golders Green Station, well laden RF430 makes the acute turn at Jack Straw's Castle prior to descending North End Way to its destination. Central Area RFs on this route still lacked passenger doors at this stage and the route number plate is still carried above the entrance. (P.Gomm collection)

STL2194 can be seen in the 1953 book of this series while still in the ownership of London Transport, at that time complete with roof mounted route number box. After sale it entered service with J.Yuille of Larkhall and later still operated with J.Clark & Sons of Dumfries. With its latest owner's name carried in the destination box, its considerate driver waits for the photograph to be taken before departure with a reasonable number of passengers who must be familiar with its unspecified destination. The bus was sold for scrap in 1959 to Watson, a dealer of Dumfries, ending a career which had commenced in July 1937. (R.Marshall)

RTL9 is seen on the 'Greyhound' stand at Streatham Common a few days before withdrawal and sale in March. This particular bus was one of two which had received RT10 roof-box bodies in 1956 it is said in error. Both these buses left London during the year, as did RTL501, removing the roof-box RTL from the capital for a while at least. A Ford Consul I is held at the traffic lights. This model was in build between 1950 and 1956. (M.Dryhurst)

TD51 waits at Downside before returning to Kingston, having just reversed into Downside Close. This deviation from the main 215 route, which served Ripley, had been introduced in 1954. Such was the rural nature of the route that a five mile an hour speed limit was applied in negotiating Downside Bridge across the River Mole on leaving Church Cobham. The peace and quiet of this country scene, whilst still a relative backwater, nowadays must suffer from background traffic noise from the M25 which passes by a short distance to the south. (F.W.Ivey)

Bird's Commercial Motors at Stratford-upon-Avon was visited by many photographers during the period ex-London RT family vehicles were being sold for further passenger service. In this line up from left to right are RT154, RT426 and RT174. These three vehicles were destined for Bradford Corporation later in the year where they received fleet numbers 401, 424 and 412 respectively. (J.Gascoine)

On 11th October and with the earliest type of 'Pay As You Enter, Exact Fare Please' notice in the upper nearside windscreen, RF608 has arrived at Hertford Bus Station on Route 308A with blinds reset for its next journey to Little Berkhampstead, as London Transport then spelt the village. Several other country Area routes had changed over to one-person operation on 11th July 1956 and the 308 and 308A were included although this RF had only been converted for this type of operation in October 1957. RF29, which is following, is in use on the hourly Green Line service 715A to London, Marble Arch via Tottenham, another innovation which commenced with the 11th July 1956 programme. (A.R.Packer)

The route 73A, on which Hounslow's RT2026 is working, lasted just over three months, taking to the road on 26th November of the year under review and being withdrawn after 3rd March 1958. Although mentioned in an amendment leaflet, it never actually made it on to a London Bus Map. It was the result of the withdrawal of Route 33 between Hammersmith and Hounslow and the A suffix indicated the Monday to Friday workings covering the Hounslow to Richmond section which deviated from the main 73 by running to Lower Mortlake Road, Stanmore Road to terminate. After March 1959 journeys on the main 73 service covered its withdrawal. (R.Wellings)

Route 321A diverted from the main 321 route to Uxbridge at Rickmansworth to terminate at the Berry Lane Estate. On 28th December RT3868 stops beside the Watford Post Office before continuing its journey to Luton. At its second overhaul, which took place in February of the following year, the bus was outshopped in Central Area colours, severing its association with the Country Area dating from its initial entry into service in September 1950 at Swanley Junction garage. (A.R.Packer)

The 1945 Daimler CWA6 chassis of ex-D53 provides the basis for Southend Corporation Transport fleet number 273 with lowbridge Massey bodywork of 1954 manufacture. Seen near the centre of this popular seaside town, it works on Route 6 to Newington Avenue. Almost every possible window is open which perhaps is a comment not only on the weather, but also on the superior ventilation that half-drop windows would have provided. The Corporation purchased thirteen of the D class buses all of which were rebodied prior to entering service in the familiar blue and cream livery first introduced around the outbreak of World War II. (D.F.Parker)

On 11th October this view of GS29 at Ewhurst shows to good advantage the rear end lines produced by the bodybuilder, Eastern Coachworks, which were almost identical to those of a Metro-Cammell bodied RF. Centrally placed emergency rear door and the two headed, somewhat confusing, turning arrows above the registration plate are characteristically London Transport inspired, to which 1954 requirement reflectors have been added. All one man operated buses and coaches were fitted with a reversing light in the course of the spread of this type of operation. (A.G.Newman)

Last minute shoppers in abundance throng the pavement in Romford town centre on 24th December as RT2122 pauses on its journey to Collier Row, White Hart. Hornchurch garage's responsibility for the route was transferred to the new North Street, Romford premises upon it being brought into operation on 12th August 1953 and at the time RTL class buses continued to operate the route. RTs replaced the Leylands in January 1954. The 'hop on a bus' campaign of London Transport advertised on the side of the bus could hardly have foreseen buses in the area some thirty years later calling themselves 'East London hoppas'! (A.R.Packer)

An early post-war Vauxhall car pulls out to overtake Saunders bodied RT3269 which is itself about to pull into the stream of traffic at Kensal Rise. The bus had re-entered service at Gillingham Street, Victoria garage from its February overhaul and is adorned with front advertising for the Air France service to Nice, described as the 'Riviera Express', reminiscent of the pre-war practice of the railway groups. (M.Dryhurst)

GS14 appears to have run down to the bus station at Hertford on 11th October on some errand from the garage at Fairfax Road. Although withdrawn from service in December 1967 this vehicle was nevertheless transferred to London Country Bus Services on 1st January 1970, not to be disposed of until April 1971 when it found further passenger use with Tillingbourne Valley before moving into the preservation movement in 1976. (A.R.Packer)

Standing in the vicinity of Belfast City Hall on 28th September, ex-D185 waits departure for Sydenham on Route 75 - a route number and destination not out of place in south east London, although London's Albert Bridge is not suitable for buses. The one piece driver's windscreen and reduced saloon ventilation of the Harkness bodywork now carried appear retrograde when compared to the original Park Royal body. However, the pleasing lines of the body admirably disguise the 1946 built Daimler CWA6 chassis. The ladies on the lower deck appear to be enjoying a joke at the photographer's expense. (J.C.Gillham)

With the Queens Building at London Airport Central as a backdrop, red liveried RM2 leaves for its journey to Wandsworth Bridge on Route 91. To anyone who knows only the present scenario at London Airport, this scene of tranquillity must be totally incomprehensible. It just shows how air travel has developed and the world become smaller. (J.Thomson)

On 2nd March Hendon garaged RT3395 stands in Golders Green station forecourt before departing on Route 183 to Northwood Station. Upon receiving an overhaul in June of the following year the RT3 body would be discarded in favour of an RT8 example, more appropriate to the fleet number. The side advertisement is extremely local to the 183 route, offering ladies coiffure in Golders Green and Hendon. (W.R.Legg)

Traversing Praed Street, Paddington sometime during November, Riverside garaged RTL1432 carries a respectable number of passengers which include a gentleman drawing on his cigarette while seated in the front of the upper deck. One is tempted to enquire whether this is a Woodbine, as advertised on the front panelling. A further overhaul in 1964 no doubt helped in the bus continuing in passenger service through to the last year of operation of the class in 1968. Currently in use on Route 27 the bus carries running plates R1 and heads towards Highgate, Archway Station. (A.R.Packer)

This area of the High Street at Uxbridge is pedestrianised nowadays but previously buses, which had commenced their journey at the side entrance of the Underground station, also served the stop at the front which was accessed by this lay-by. The wiring for trolleybuses was erected in 1953 and used in the following year as a temporary terminus for the 607 when road works prevented them reaching their normal terminus at Fray's River. The wires were subsequently left in place but rarely used. TD95 picks up more passengers before a journey through Colnbrook and Staines to Laleham. This bus nowadays is kept in superb condition at the Cobham Bus Museum. (M.Dryhurst)

RT294 has been treated to two overhauls, having first entered service in February 1948, but at this stage it still carries a body similar to that originally fitted. On its next visit to Aldenham it re-entered service with an RT8 type body ensuring its longevity with London Transport, not being disposed of until July 1977. Here at Crystal Palace on 15th November, time has almost approached for departure on a short journey to Charing Cross over Route 3. (A.R.Packer)

Standing at the Parkway, New Addington terminus RT1708 awaits departure time for its journey to Thornton Heath High Street on Route 130A. This route commenced on 6th October 1954 and ran until October 1978 when it was a victim of another round of changes in the routes on the Croydon - New Addington corridor which at the time of writing awaits the possibly final steadying influence of Tramlink. The bus is interesting since at its final overhaul in October 1969 it was to acquire the body from RT2776 with the distinctive ventilators in the front dome dating from its 1952 trip to America. (A.Mortimer)

In December 1957 CRL4 had completed its initial spell of use on Route 721 from London Road, Romford garage. It was then transferred to High Wycombe for driver training with further familiarisation at Reigate before entry into service on Route 711. In January it is seen with running plates HE53 southbound at Baker Street Station. On 1st May it entered Chiswick Works not returning to revenue service until July when its next use would be on the Windsor - Tunbridge Wells route 704. (A.R.Packer)

RT254 catches the rays of the setting sun one warm evening in June, as it is about to cross Greenford Road on the ascent into the Broadway. Additional masking around the roof route number box appears to have been added to the otherwise standard RT3 body. Overhauled the following month, this RT would never again be quite the same as it was thereafter fitted with later non roof-box style bodies. (M.Dryhurst)

RT4625 had re-entered service garaged at Norbiton and carrying body number 8497 after receiving an overhaul in March 1957. It did not venture further afield until scheduled for another overhaul in March 1961 after which Hornchurch was to be its new home. Here in Cromwell Road, Kingston on 27th December it has arrived after a Chessington, Copt Gilders to Kingston journey on Route 265. Some readers will be able to remember many of the names of the cast involved with the production of 'Cinderella' at the Chiswick Empire, although nowadays it would hardly be likely that the show would be advertised as 'London's gayest pantomime', such is the change in our use of language. (A.R.Packer)

The chassis and easily recognisable Park Royal body of RT2776, originally delivered in January 1952, remained married together until its final overhaul in January 1969. The added ventilation grilles provided for its trip to the U.S.A. always remained in place. Having attained six years passenger use it is now seen in August keeping well clear of the temporarily constructed walkway erected while building work progresses in New Oxford Street. The bus was garaged at Forest Gate for most of its first nine years of service and is here in use on Route 25 on a journey which will terminate at Becontree Heath. (M.Dryhurst)

Epping garage yard sometime during December reveals Green Line liveried RT3242 parked with route blinds for use on Route 396 and carrying running plates EP202, which suggests a supplementary schedule more normally associated with Green Line. In fact, the bus may have worked back in service from Harlow after such a stint on the 718. Normally a resident of London Road, Romford garage its temporary custodians have taken the easy option by fitting a side or rear blind in the via box aperture. (A.R.Packer)

On 30th November of the year under review the Sunday service on Routes 43 and 143 was replaced by extending 133 north from the City to Hendon Central Station. This was a reversal of pre-war practice when 43 and 143 provided the Sunday service south of London Bridge. Brixton's RT2050 lays over on 28th December at the roundabout then in situ in front of Hendon Central Station before making the long journey to South Croydon. The bus had been overhauled recently in October. (A.R.Packer)

The 384A route operated a couple of Monday to Friday journeys and a two-hourly service on Saturday afternoons which turned off the main 384 at Dane End and ran to Great Munden, turning at the schools. Nowadays the village is only served by one Monday return journey on Richmond's route 21 and a Post Bus which rambles between Ware and Buntingford. On 11th October RF632 is waiting for a driver from Hertford garage to emerge from Fairfax Road behind the bus to continue its journey. (A.R.Packer)

RT327 in use on Route 29 is one of Palmers Green's weekend contribution on the route which was chiefly serviced by Potters Bar and West Green garages. After 26th November Palmers Green's allocation was further limited to just five buses on Saturdays. Overhauled in January of the following year the bus was fitted then with a non-roof box body which assured its longevity until March 1972. Note the old set of blinds in use, even a destination with the word 'only', which are still surviving in March of the year under review. (A.R.Packer)

RT571, last overhauled in 1956, appears two years later to have lost its sheen when seen in service on Route 36 and garaged at Peckham. With few passengers the driver waits the conductor's bell before departing the compulsory bus stop in Grosvenor Gardens on Sunday 23rd March to continue its journey to Hither Green Station. The annual Ideal Home Exhibition held at Olympia is the subject of the side advertisement but only six days remain if you wish to visit it. (A.R.Packer)

Lowland Motor Services of Snettleston acquired ex-RT1501 in October 1957 repainting it into their colour scheme and allocating fleet number 43 before entry into service. On a dismal 4th January and riding the tram tracks and road setts it is obviously in passenger service although route apertures not covered in paint still lack route blinds. Initially entering service with London Transport in November 1949 in Central Area livery, it operated form Willesden garage. In December 1953 it received its one and only overhaul and in March 1956 received Country Area livery for use at Windsor and Watford High Street garages before withdrawal from service in November 1956. Subsequent storage followed at Shepherds Bush garage until the bus was disposed of in April 1957. (A.J.Douglas)

Cricklewood garaged RF10 is seen in August on a Private Hire charter turning into City Road at the Angel, Islington road junction in heavy traffic. The original twenty five strong private hire coach RF variant had been reduced to fifteen when the other members were repainted into Green Line livery in 1956. All had received this drab colour scheme, having lost their attractive green and grey livery with red lining out. This RF can be seen nowadays in preserved condition at rallies, happily returned to its original colour scheme. (Michael Dryhurst)

T792 is seen at the War Memorial, Rainham with route blind showing 375 Rainham Ferry and Rainham Crossing, a display intended for the short workings at the other end of this short route. Transferred to East Grinstead in January 1960 and Tring in the following October, final withdrawal of this bus occurred in December 1960 after a little over twelve years operation with London Transport including the period from September 1957 when it was housed at Grays garage. Fortunately the bus is one of the few of the type which is now preserved. (M.Rooum)

The last operator to use this 'pre-war' RT in passenger service was Anderson Bros. of Evenwood, County Durham. On 12th October it is seen in very poor condition at Bird's Commercial Motors' premises, Stratford-upon-Avon. Thankfully the rear registration plate is still attached together with its previous owner's fleet name 'Blue Belle' showing in the destination box, confirming it to be RT27 having reached the yard in April. (A.R.Packer)

November 25th was the last day on which the 14T12 type bus was used on Route 211 which operated between Ealing Broadway and Greenford. T744 is seen at the Ealing, Haven Green terminal on that day. Tomorrow RFs transferred in from Sidcup would be used and the crew would no longer need to stand on the pavement to have a chat between journeys. The bus seen here was included in the first shipment of the type to Ceylon in December of the year now under review. (J.C.Gillham)

RT3440 with running plates EP3 stands at the entrance to Epping garage sometime in December. This was a favoured spot by bus photographers who visited Epping and while the passenger shelters gained added splash panels over the years, it still remains a fairly rudimentary environment in which to wait for your bus. (A.R.Packer)

From the vantage point of Hornsey Lane road bridge high above the Archway Road two very different road users climb the hill as they head north out of London - Foden articulated lorry and RT3018, which now carries an RT3 body, numbered 2024. The bus is heading for Hampden Road at Muswell Hill on Route 43. This stretch of road was doubled in width to dual carriageway conditions in due course but here the trolleybus wiring for Routes 517, 617 and 609 is still in place. (M.Dryhurst)

RF202 was to be the longest serving member of the class in regular passenger service with LT, LCBS and successor companies. Continuing for seven years after previous members of the class were last in revenue earning capacity. It is seen at Gravesend on 6th December waiting to depart for Ascot on Green Line service 701 just six years into its illustrious existence. Nowadays the vehicle is preserved in its September 1966 modernised condition but unfortunately carries replacement registration number AVS678. (A.R.Packer)

RT951 is seen picking up passengers at Clapham Common on 22nd November while in use on Route 118 on a running in journey to its home at Streatham garage. Since its last overhaul in December 1956 the bus had been garaged at Croydon, only being transferred to Streatham in April but before the year end it was further transferred to Barking to continue its service. (A.R.Packer)

In Redhill town centre outside a well stocked branch of Dewhurst the butchers, RT4727 does brisk business on 20th September, having initially entered service in March of the year under review. Rather surprisingly the bus is still devoid of any advertising to spoil its exterior paintwork and with the unspoilt front and rear wheel trims, hides the fact that it is four years old. The trunk route 405 operated between West Croydon station and Horsham via Crawley and had its origins in East Surrey Route S5, which itself came out of an unnumbered route starting in 1911. (A.R.Packer)

725J had started life as STL186, entering service with the LPTB in July 1933 having been ordered by the LGOC, whose fleetname it originally carried. Withdrawn from service in September 1947, it was selected for conversion to a service vehicle. It emerged as a 5-ton tower wagon in red livery in May 1948 and continued in its new role through to April 1960. With differing front mudguards prominent in the portion of the front lower deck of its STL1 bodywork which was retained, it waits a further call to service near the end of a distinguished career. (J.A.S.Hambley collection)

Since October 1956 RF21 has carried Green Line livery and fleet names and stands outside East Grinstead garage resting between trips on Route 708. Allocated to Two Waters garage for the first half of the year under review, it carries EG plates having stayed overnight at the southern end of the route. Converted from its private hire coach function, which had commenced in June 1951, it now serves as a Green Line coach but in 1962 the whole batch of shorter RFs used in this way were withdrawn from service. (D.W.K.Jones)

RTL178 has travelled from its home garage of Camberwell to Dunton Green for passenger use on the special service on Route 410 between Bromley North Station and the Biggin Hill Air Display. Running plates DG257 are carried for its task. With two overhauls having already been afforded the bus would only receive one more before disposal in May 1964. (A.Mortimer)

RT3113 had initially entered service at Putney Bridge garage in April 1950 and saw further use at Bromley and Croydon before arriving at Norbiton garage following a November 1957 overhaul. Park Royal body number 1469, originally carried by RT220, now graces the chassis which inevitably sealed the vehicle's fate but not before its final passenger carrying days at Muswell Hill garage were completed. After long time storage it was disposed of in November 1963. Here on 27th December it is parked amid the familiar surrounding of Kingston railway station terminus. (A.R.Packer)

RF679 had first entered service within the Country Area as a 41 seat bus in October 1953 carrying body number 8856 and classification 2RF2/2. In July of the year under review it was converted for one man operation with seating reduced to 39 and reclassified 2RF5/1. Just two months later it entered Aldenham for overhaul, being outshopped with a 10/58 date and fitted with body number 8847. In this condition it is seen operating from Addlestone garage with route blind wound for Route 427 and carrying discreet pay as you enter instructions fixed to the nearside front windscreen. (P.J.Malsher)

Merton garage always housed RT4277 when it wore Central Area livery from its entry into service in June 1953 through to July 1956, the date of its first overhaul. It re-emerged then in Country Area colours which it retained through to disposal in September 1963. By then it had seen passenger service at Staines, Watford High Street and Garston. Here on 28th December it is in use on Route 311 in Clarendon Road, Watford as it journeys to Chilcott Road. (A.R.Packer)

An impressive array of AEC buses and coaches are parked within the Progressive Coaches base at Cambridge on a particularly sunny day during the year under review. Three of the remaining four 2RT2s from the original batch of five purchased in January 1956 keep two STLs acquired earlier company with two of the single deck 'Regal' model from the Southall factory. The buses providing most interest to readers are, from left to right, ex-RT40, front entrance STL971 purchased in October 1953, STL2117 a 1955 purchase and still retaining its front route boxes, while furthest from the camera ex-RT76 and ex-RT84 complete the picture. (R.Hobbs)

RTW3 lays over at Kensal Rise one Saturday in March before departing on the long run through the West End and City to reach its destination at Hackney Wick. Although one of the pioneers of the eight feet wide class at Tottenham, the bus was garaged at Willesden after February 1951 and remained there through three overhauls before being transferred to Chalk Farm in June 1965. An offside view of the bus appears in the 1954 book of this series showing it in use on Route 18, both of which routes were associated with the garage for many years. (M.Dryhurst)

The date is 31st May, the first day of operation for the People's League for the Defence of Freedom bus services in the absence of London Transport. FT5702 stands at the Wilton Road entrance to Victoria Station with signwriting and various paper stickers, including a torn example above the front indicators which should read 'To help busless London'. Having been acquired direct from Tynemouth and District just days previously, the bus dates from 1946 and is an AEC Regent with Weymann bodywork. This looks like a publicity opportunity by the People's League before actual operation commenced. (A.R.Packer)

Although really outside the scope with regard to the subject matter of this series of books, it was felt necessary to include a selection of the vehicles which operated during the seven week long total London Transport bus strike in May and June of the year under review. DBC224, an ex-Leicester City Transport AEC Renown gathers momentum as it traverses the junction of Hobart Place with Grosvenor Place. The notice under the canopy announces a flat fare of 6d. indicating the photograph was taken after 13th June by which time licenses had been obtained from London Transport. Previously the services had been free. (Roy Hobbs)

GCD688, a Leyland TD7 fitted with Park Royal 52 seat bodywork, was new in March 1941 as Crosville Motor Services Ltd. M126. It was the last numbered of a batch M111 through to M126 which had been ordered by Southdown Motor Services Ltd. but diverted due to wartime conditions. Most of the sixteen were rebodied during their years with Crosville with operator built bodies. After disposal earlier in the year under review the bus eventually passed to E.D.Martell and B.Goddard of London WC1 who, after a few weeks of operation in London, disposed of the bus for further service by A.J.Boakes (Camden Coaches) of Sevenoaks. Here it is seen in June as it passes the bus shelters outside East Croydon Station while in use on the League's Route 2 between Croydon and Addington. (Roy Hobbs)

Originally the property of the East Kent Road Car Company, JG9956 is a Leyland Tiger TS8 fitted with Park Royal bodywork. It is at Roehampton on the League's Route 3 to Hammersmith towards the end of the period during which a small number of buses and coaches provided so much variety. (D.W.K.Jones)

The south end of Park Lane presents a very different picture to present day users having had its fair share of redevelopment and road widening schemes during the second half of the century. In use on Route 1 operated during the duration of the strike, ex-Thames Valley Services 429 is a combination of Bristol K6A chassis and utility Strachan low height bodywork. With the Karrier Bantam tractor and trailer unit about to overtake the pair make an unusual and interesting sight at this location. (Roy Hobbs)

FTD618 was new to Lytham St.Annes Corporation in February 1944 as their No.23. It is a Daimler CWA6 fitted with Duple bodywork and is now owned by Cyril Green Enterprises of South West London, having been obtained through Max Speed Transportation, a local dealer. Now on loan to the People's League for the Defence of Freedom, it still carries its former owner's route blind although 'Free Ride at your own Risk' stickers are now displayed. The bus is heading north up Charing Cross Road, which was not on any of the League's routes, so it may be that the 'Depot' destination display was deliberate. (Roy Hobbs)

Two of the League's buses in operation on Route 1 are seen in Grosvenor Gardens. On the right of the picture beside the bus stop 'For Buses to Victoria Station Only' BFN934, a Leyland TD7 with Crosville built bodywork, had been one of a batch of ten ordered by East Kent Motor Services in 1940 but diverted. This example became M108 in the Crosville fleet. At this time it was in the ownership of the same organisation as GCD688 seen elsewhere in this book. FTD612 on the opposite side of the road presents a little problem, as its registration has not been found belonging to a bus although FTD617 and 618 were both operated in the Capital during the strike and one wonders if its registration is incorrect. (Roy Hobbs)

In this view taken in June at Grosvenor Gardens, Victoria, two six wheelers with different chassis and bodywork combinations are eyed by a gathering of pedestrians and prospective passengers. Nearer the camera is DUC904, a 1937 built Leyland TS7T chassis fitted with Duple bodywork. Originally delivered new to the City Coach Company Ltd. as their fleet number LT28, it was a well-known performer on the Wood Green to Southend on Sea route. It passed to Westcliff on Sea Motor Services upon the sale of the City business to the British Transport Commission and after disposal led a chequered career. The double deck in the background dates from 1940, being an AEC Renown carrying MCCW bodywork initially delivered to Leicester City Transport as their number 330. Both operate on the League service Number 1 from Victoria to Marble Arch. (Roy Hobbs)

ABE335, a Leyland TS originally owned by the Lincolnshire Road Car Company, is now operated by the People's League for the Defence of Freedom on their Route 6, which ran between the Oval and Thornton Heath. Seen as it heads south through Norbury it is interesting to note two cyclists. Obviously this means of transport came into its own for a period and also of significance is the liberal car parking opportunities on one of London's busiest trunk roads, the A23. (Roy Hobbs)

Some time during the month of June all-Crossley built HTC615, which is an SC42/3 model fitted with bus type bodywork with seating for 36, is about to turn out of Friends Road, South Croydon. It is engaged on the League's Route 2 which operated between Addington and South Croydon. The bus was owned at the time by the same organisation as FTD618 seen elsewhere within the pages of this volume. (D.W.K.Jones)

RT230 received an overhaul in September of the year under review, re-entering service with bodywork of a later style, but prior to this it is viewed during March with the RT3 type which it had carried since first entering service in November 1947. The familiar Wembley background is seen during one of its quieter periods and the RT carries one of the earliest style of post-war via point blinds, which crammed as much information in as was practical. (A.R.Packer)

On 6th April RT1862 on Route 52 has another left hand turn to complete before reaching its destination at Victoria Station. On the left of the picture RT1668 has departed from the same terminal point and is about to turn right into Grosvenor Gardens at the beginning of its long haul to Becontree Heath. The body, numbered 1729, carried by this bus had been fitted in September 1957 upon the vehicle's overhaul at Aldenham. Acquired by Red Rover in November 1964 it would then suffer some modifications. (W.R.Legg)

On 5th July deserted TD101 is parked in the Edgware Station forecourt awaiting its next journey on Route 240A with running plates EW1. The bus is still making use of the route stencil holder above the saloon doorway at a time when some of the type had lost the fixture and on others it had fallen into disuse. The single deckers traditionally used the outer perimeter of this small bus station while double deckers, such as the 142 in the background, parked in the centre. (A.R.Packer)

Upton Park's RTW85 is seen in Praed Street, Paddington on Route 23A to Becontree Heath just a few weeks before the service was withdrawn. This was a Sunday only route which up until 1949 had been numbered 163 and which finally ran on 23rd November without any direct replacement leaving other services to cover various sections of the route between Ladbroke Grove and Becontree Heath via Holborn. (A.R.Packer)

Former RT1519 was acquired by Red Rover, Aylesbury in October 1956, given fleet number 2 and the route number box removed from the front dome. Now wearing the much darker red of its new owner but in a similar application to London Transport style, it takes refuge in its operator's yard at Aylesbury before being recalled for use. It eventually completed more years' public service in and around Aylesbury than when used in passenger service at Croydon and Leyton.

(J.A.S.Hambley)

An exchange of passengers takes place at Surrey Docks on RF514's short journey between South Bermondsey and New Cross, Clifton Rise on Route 202. This fleet number had originally been carried by a Country Area bus, which in March 1956 was renumbered RF295 and converted to Green Line configuration in the following month. Meanwhile at the same time the original RF295 with registration number MLL932 was renumbered RF514 as seen in this view taken on 15th November. (A.R.Packer)

GS4 had initially entered passenger service in December 1953 garaged at Amersham being called into Aldenham in March 1956 for its first overhaul. It re-entered service at Chelsham where it remained until being withdrawn from passenger use in October 1962. On 20th September is it seen on Route 485 which ran between Edenbridge and Westerham via Crockham Hill. The small group of routes, 464, 465 and 485 were converted to GS bus operation in October 1953 losing them in favour of RFs in October 1962. (A.R.Packer)

On 3rd August RT980 pauses in London Road, Grays on a short journey to West Thurrock on Route 371B which at its fullest extent reached Rainham. If the children running behind are trying to catch the bus one hopes that the rear blind is also set to show its shortened service. (A.B.Cross)

Brake pipe hoses hang beneath the offside wheel arch with the steering lock at its maximum, which allowed a turning circle of 60 feet for this Leyland PS1 chassis. Kingston railway station can be seen behind TD112 with sister vehicle TD58 closely parked behind as they lay over on Route 216 to Staines on 27th December. The subject bus was withdrawn from service in March 1962 while, by that time, the other example had already completed several years service in Ceylon, having been withdrawn in June 1959 and exported almost immediately. (A.R.Packer)

Culling's Coaches of Claxton in Norfolk owned ex-STD96 from July 1955 through to November 1961 after which it was disposed of to Yeates Ltd. of Loughborough, Leicestershire, then operating as a dealer. However, it still remained at its previous operator's premises at Claxton, gradually deteriorating for many months after. In more prosperous times it is seen with 'Hardley and District Service' carried in the front route box. Although having lost its roof mounted indicator box it has gained a cab door. (J.A.S.Hambley collection)

RT3125 is about to be overtaken by a Morris 8 saloon, first registered in July 1938 and one of the last of a shape superseded by the much more modern looking series E of 1939. The date is Saturday 20th September and all this activity is taking place at Dorking. The bus is working as DS19, which was the single RT working on this service on Saturdays and, apart from one journey from Goodwyns Farm Estate, plied only between the town and Chart Downs Estate. The other bus, DS18, was a GS which provided the spasmodic service through to Ewhurst. This service however was cut back to Holmwood Common (Four Wents Pond) leaving the section to Ewhurst unserved after 28th October. (A.R.Packer)

Two AEC products lead with Leyland equivalents following in this scene taken on 19th April at the top of Whitehall in Trafalgar Square. Centrepiece RT4605, in service on Route 53 to Camden Town, carries a slip board on the front bulkhead advising that the route operates in close proximity to the Zoo. (W.R.Legg)

Route 333B operated daily journeys for the benefit of staff and for visitors to the Ware Park Hospital situated beside the confluence of the Rivers Rib and Lea just outside the town. At Hertford bus station on 11th October one person operated RF627 welcomes aboard a number of passengers for the short journey which included the use of the hospital's private road to reach the terminal. (A.R.Packer)

RT656 passes a structure looking as if it is part of a German prisoner of war camp in World War II rather than a police traffic light control point. The general chaos is associated with the building of the Chiswick flyover at Gunnersbury. Although with six years London Transport service still to complete, the bus is seen on Route 91 operating from its final home of Turnham Green. In this April view it is about to join the Great West Road for a journey to London Airport Central, while surprisingly fitted with a route number stencil in the front nearside pillar fitting, something of a rarity in the year now under review. (M.Dryhurst)

RT3708 rests in St.Mary's Square, Hitchin on 22nd March while working the Tuesday and Saturday market day Route 811 between here and Longmeadow. As the blind shows the route, which had been introduced the previous October, ran non-stop from Hitchin to the White Lion at Stevenage. It lasted until October 1960 by which time the shopping facilities at Stevenage had developed to negate the purpose of the route. The bus first entered service in May 1953 wearing Central Area livery at Enfield. Overhauled in May 1956 it re-entered service at Addlestone in Country Area colours which it retained until October 1965 when again it was outshopped from overhaul in red livery and allocated to Sidcup. (A.R.Packer)

Christmas Eve finds RT4584 working Route 129 at Claybury Broadway. Although fairly short one feels that a more detailed blind display would have usefully shown that Barkingside and Gants Hill were served en-route. Indeed on 30th November the route had taken over the Sunday afternoon hospital journeys beyond Ilford to Little Heath from the 25A. Seven Kings had received this RT only days earlier from North Street, Romford. It remained at AP until its May 1960 overhaul when it re-entered service at Peckham. (A.R.Packer)

Turning at Staines West Station on 19th July, RLH12 carries WY10 running plates for its use on Route 436A. This bus was one of two members of the class which managed never to be transferred away from Addlestone. It entered service in June 1950 and though passing through three overhauls in May 1954, March 1958 and February 1963 it was always returned to service at Addlestone. Eventually delicensed in June 1965 it was tucked away in the same location to await disposal, which happened in February 1966 when it was despatched to Dagenham Motors of London SE6 for immediate resale. In this scene it is kept company by an Austin saloon and either a Bentley or Rolls Royce with specialist bodywork. (A.R.Packer)

This picture could be titled 'A Study in Failure'. The scene is Ongar Station, then on the Central Line and the bored looking driver operator has the lonely privilege of working one of the final journeys through to this point on Route 381. Two Saturday journeys had been extended on from Toothill starting 16th October 1957 but, lacking any custom, they were withdrawn after 18th January of the year under review. The Underground makes a brave attempt to encourage passengers through the sale of Red Rover tickets, which from this distant outpost represented good value. However, even the trains were to disappear altogether in the 1990s. GS37 was garaged at Epping from October 1957 through to June 1959, having first entered service at Dorking in December 1953. (John Lines collection)

Having arrived at Hertford bus station on 11th October, a journey to Nup End by way of Route 329 is next scheduled for GS44 which already shows the muddy conditions of the Hertfordshire lanes. One of the more travelled members of the class, including a period of staff bus duties, the bus was eventually disposed of in 1968 to Stanley Hugh Leach Ltd. of Yeading, Middlesex only to be scrapped in 1972. Also to be seen in the picture is a Morris Commercial one ton lorry to the left and an Austin 12/16 to the right. (A.R.Packer)

Operating further down the Thames Estuary than is usual, RT4192 nearest the camera and RT3605 wait at Pitsea Station on a Railway Emergency Service on 16th February. The paper sticker carried in the rearmost lower deck window of RT4192 seeks men and women conductors although any potential recruit in this neighbourhood would probably prefer to work for Eastern National. (F.Church)

Red Rover, Aylesbury operated a sizeable fleet of ex-London Transport buses for many years which included a number of RTs. A familiar sight on routes operated by Leyton garage for its entire working life in the capital, RT423 still wears the London livery as it serves the Buckinghamshire market town and immediate countryside. Following in the distance round the road works is earlier variant RT31 (Red Rover fleet number 8) which has had its roof box removed. Note at the far right of the picture the London Transport bus stop now temporarily out of commission with E plates for Green Line services 706 and 707. (F.W.Ivey)

The remains of T668 languish in the Bird's Commercial Motors yard at Stratford upon Avon surrounded by desolation and lifeless trees. Careful inspection reveals the tree line on the horizon to be in full foliage, which suggest those nearer the camera suffer pollution from oil and metal poison. After the years spent with American Red Cross, as seen in the 1939-45 volume of this series of books, this T class vehicle re-entered Green Line service in June 1946 garaged at Dunton Green. Further passenger use at a number of garages ended when in October 1956 it was disposed. (J.A.S. Hambley collection)

At Putney Bridge Station RTL824, a resident of the garage situated just across the River Thames, is seen in company with Merton garaged RT4714 parked a safe distance along the road. The lead bus will depart for the ultimate destination of Epsom Station with North Cheam, Priory Road the shorter journey for the RT. The date is 1st November and by the end of the month Putney Bridge garage would be no longer used and Chelverton Road would take over this working. (J.Gascoine collection)

Red Rover have obviously pressed RT212 into service quickly, still retaining its previous operator's livery, advertisements and fleet number. The bus is seen in Kingsbury Square, Aylesbury during December. It had been withdrawn from service by London Transport, having last seen passenger service at Norwood garage in April. After storage at several locations in delicensed condition it eventually left for Bird's Commercial Motors in November. It still carries the original Park Royal bodywork with which it first entered service in November 1947 at Potters Bar garage. (M.Dryhurst)

Red liveried RT2339 is seen on 16th December having just passed the Maidstone & District local offices and garage at Gravesend. Only a side route blind is fitted in the front via box to suffice for the temporary loan from Plumstead to Northfleet garage and the vehicle's use on Route 496 between Northfleet and the Kings Farm Estate at Gravesend. (A.R.Packer)

Acquired by D.R.& B.McKechnie & N.Cole, who traded as 'Cream Bus Service', in February 1957 ex-RT1472 looks splendid in its new paint scheme. Alongside, FTL439 is a Duple bodied SB new in January 1952 to the Cream Bus Service and both vehicles were later operated by Barton Transport Ltd. after their take-over in February 1961 together with twenty other vehicles. To the right of the picture a classic saloon car can be seen manufactured by the SS concern, the forerunner of Jaguar. (A.Mortimer)

Two of the six TDs supplied by Norbiton garage to work weekday Route 264 are seen at Kingston railway station on 27th December. TD58 in the upper picture carries the old style of single deck route blind while TD32, below, carries the more modern version. While clarity may have been achieved, the loss of information is very evident. British Rail encourage use of the train to London at a return fare of 4/2d - not quite 21p in modern money - while the telephone box is of the type which now form a strange sort of sculpture in part of the town centre not so far away from these scenes. (Both pictures A.R.Packer)

During March, RT195 traverses Balfe Street at Kings Cross as it heads for Caledonian Road to take up duty again on Route 14 to Putney passing an Austin A40 'Devon' light van. After its spell garaged at Holloway, this RT entered Aldenham for a further overhaul to be outshopped in August with a non-roof box body, which helped ensure its longevity through to 1972 when it was finally disposed of as scrap. (M.Dryhurst)

On a Sunday during September RT4604 is seen working a special rail replacement service outside the Westbourne Park Metropolitan Line station. The driver of the Alperton garaged bus is in conversation with an inspector in a scene lacking much other activity. (A.R.Packer)

The Cream Bus Services of Stamford purchased former RT1404 in March 1957 via the dealer, Bird's of Stratford upon Avon. It had been used in passenger service at Watford High Street garage all through its comparatively short time in the ownership of London Transport. This ran from January 1949 to February 1957 and the bus enjoyed an overhaul in April 1953. At a rather bleak bus station the superbly presented Craven bodied bus works on the route between Stamford and Peterborough. (J.A.S.Hambley collection)

RT389 still carries an older five line via point blind and a destination, Harrow Weald Garage, with the qualifying word 'only', while RT1763 furthest from the camera is fitted with four lines of route information for its full journey to Rayners Lane L.T.Station. The date is 5th July and Edgware is the resting-place for the identical looking buses. Identical that is unless you are an expert in the construction methods for the different roofs fitted. (A.R.Packer)

One can almost imagine the ghost of a 15T13 appearing as RF700 is viewed, parked in the identical spot as T776 featured on page 112 of the 1951 book of this series. The date here is 28th December and the background almost appears to have been caught up in a time warp. However, it is a one person operated 39 seat Metro-Cammell bodied AEC Regal IV which waits to run over Route 322 to Hemel Hempstead and the illusion is shattered. (A.R.Packer)

RT1535 occupies centre stage at a busy Golders Green terminus on 28th December before leaving on the shorter journey to Pinner carried out by alternate buses on the 183. The driver's seat is clearly visible and is still one of the high backed variety originally fitted to the RTs. Two Metro-Cammell bodied RTLs, distinguishable by their narrow central band and thicker upper moulding, wait further use on Route 28, parked beneath the leafless skeleton of a well matured tree. (A.R.Packer)

It was the advance of one man operation, coupled with reduced schedules which sealed the fate of most of the T type single deckers in the Country Area. With only a small number being required by the end of 1958, surplus examples found further use in and around Kingston with the Central Area or as staff buses scattered far and wide throughout the system. T786 is seen at the Hampton Court Station terminal of route 206 before departure to Claygate, Holroyd Road on what appears to be a pleasant day, although not many tourists are in evidence. Early in the following year the bus was stored at London Road, Romford garage for several months after which further passenger use at East Grinstead occurred before final withdrawal in January 1960. (J.Thomson)

Red liveried RT3915 is seen in the parking area at Ascot RaceCourse on 19th July having completed a journey on the special bus service from Staines. Normally resident at Hounslow garage it would visit Aldenham for overhaul in September and re-enter service at Streatham garage. The hoarding to the right states 'No.6 Silver Ring Car Park: 7/6d daily'. That's 37½p for all day parking, how times have changed. (A.R.Packer)

Having entered passenger service in February of the year now under review after its enforced storage since delivery in October 1954, RTL1600 is seen in East India Dock Road, Poplar on Route 108A. The blind is set for Eltham, Southend Crescent but the bus appears to be heading northwards in the direction of Bromley-by-Bow. The nasty dent in the side of the front dome panel might indicate a close encounter with the Blackwall Tunnel on one of its many trips through the winding old bore. Rather surprisingly after only one overhaul in October 1961, when it returned to service fitted with body number 4713, this RTL was disposed of in June 1965. It was at that time the highest numbered to suffer this fate and only had seven years of passenger service with London Transport. (F.W.Ivey)

TD35 stands in Cromwell Road, Kingston towards the end of December with route blind wound ready for the next trip to Downside on the 215A service which had been introduced in June 1954 and lasted through to December 1967. By comparison the bus was used in passenger service from May 1949 through to October 1962, an almost identical life span, although not concurrent, for both to be used by the travelling public. (A.R.Packer)

The route number 48 had lain dormant after 24th October 1939 until it was re-introduced on 6th January with the sixth stage of the tram replacement scheme. It used the same roads as tram service 48 between West Norwood and the City. The route was withdrawn on 20th August being covered at the southern end by an extension of the 42. Camberwell's RTL770 heads for Cannon Street hotly pursued out of Walworth Road by RTL1355 on Route 171. (A.M.Wright)

With a profusion of greenery in the old coal yard bordering Clifton Terrace as a backdrop, RF528 waits departure from Finsbury Park on 12th July to Golders Green Station by way of Route 210. Originally starting life as RF309 in April 1953, it exchanged fleet numbers in March 1956 with the original Country Area RF528 in a programme which ensured coaches and buses were kept in their respective numerical batches. (A.R.Packer)

Still in smart condition despite having entered service four years previously, GS76 is seen in Broad Street at Chesham in the last week of December. Buses with a stand time in excess of four minutes were not allowed to wait at Chesham Broadway and Route 316 vehicles were required to return north, loop round Bellingdon Road and Sunnyside Road and lay over in Broad Street just south of Eskdale Avenue before returning to the Broadway for the next journey. Although the bumper bar is now painted on this bus, the radiator surround has not been similarly treated although undoubtedly this will change after its imminent first overhaul. In 1964 the bus moved to Tillingbourne Valley Services Ltd. and after further use as a mobile caravan it moved into the preservation movement in June 1978. (A.R.Packer)

The Monday to Saturday Route 4A was one of the casualties of the first stage of the Central Area bus cuts and last operated on 19th August. Route 179 was extended from Farringdon Street to Finsbury Park to cover the loss but prior to the change RT502 is seen on 12th July with the familiar Finsbury Park Station background. It is destined for Clapham Common, Old Town which shows it to be a peak hour working, despite the strange lack of people. The off peak destination was Elephant & Castle. (A.R.Packer)

This view of the Corbets Tey terminus was taken on 3rd August, a fortnight before such a shot would become impossible. Route 249, represented by RT430, and 86A, represented by RT3314 were both withdrawn on 20th August. Green Line Route 722 however would continue for a few more years to turn here at the 'Huntsman and Hounds' public house. RT3245 is the vehicle waiting to depart for Aldgate down a Green Line route which can hardly be described as green. The RT on the right of the trio is now preserved. (A.B.Cross)

At the King's Arms, Westerham a Vauxhall E series saloon car with a Bedford OB coach carrying Duple Vista bodywork are to be seen behind RLH39 which is about to continue its journey to Reigate with the driver ready to let off the handbrake. This bus would spend its entire passenger service with London Transport operating from Godstone garage, only venturing outside the immediate territory to make two visits to Aldenham for overhaul. It was subsequently exported to mainland USA where at least forty of the class of seventy-six have ended up. (A.R.Packer)

RF369 departs Kingston bus station for a journey to Sutton garage by way of Route 213. The cinema adjacent has long been used as a retail outlet but the bus station, originally opened in 1928, survived until recent new developments in Cromwell Road and Fairfield have rendered its use by passengers surplus to requirements. (P.Gomm collection)

Green liveried RLH49 was soon to experience a culture shock when in April of the following year it would be repainted into Central Area livery for many more years of passenger use at Dalston garage. The back streets of Hackney Wick would be a very different environment to the North Downs traversed by Route 410 on which it is seen at Redhill on 20th September. Running plates GD12 are carried. (A.R.Packer)

A quiet moment at Victoria Station on 23rd March finds RTW289 slowly attracting patronage before departure on Route 76 to Stoke Newington. Though for many years of its passenger use this RTW resided at Tottenham, shorter spells of operation were performed earlier at Barking and later at Willesden and Walworth before its eventual sale in March 1966. Note the customary gathering of drivers and conductors by the time clocks on the right of the picture. (A.R.Packer)

RF261 is seen at Watford on 28th December working the half-hourly Green Line Route 719 to London, Victoria via Kingsbury and Willesden. Since overhaul in July 1956 body number 7643 has graced the chassis and this combination would stay together until a further visit to Aldenham in March 1960, when again it would re-enter service carrying a lower numbered body than that originally fitted. The life span of the vehicle with London Transport and later London Country Bus Services was a creditable 22½ years from June 1952 to November 1974. After that the vehicle was despatched to Wombwell Diesels for scrap. (A.R.Packer)

With the British Railways Southend Victoria station sign in the background, ex-D136 is en-route for Shoeburyness Station on Southend Corporation Route 5A. The date is 28th June and since 1954 this Daimler CWA6 chassis has carried low bridge Massey bodywork for 55 passengers in the Corporation blue and cream colours. When compared to the photograph which appears on page 24 of the 1953 book in this series, the bus looks a different product completely. New to the London Passenger Transport Board in March 1946 fitted with a Duple high bridge body; it first saw service as a Green Line vehicle before transfer to the Central Area and eventual repaint into red livery. Withdrawn in December 1953 it was then acquired by Southend who operated it until March 1963 before sale in January 1964 to the Basildon Salvage Company for scrapping. (A.R.Packer)

After completing a period of operation within the Central Area garaged at Kingston and later Norbiton, T796 departed for its final overhaul at Aldenham in August 1957. It re-emerged in October of the same year returning to its native Country Area to complete a further eighteen months passenger use before withdrawal and eventual export to Ceylon. Allocated to Grays, it is seen at Rainham Crossing on a short working of the short Route 375 down to the Ferry. This obscure little route was finally to disappear in June 1959. (R.Wellings)

With trolleybus wiring in place overhead and a backdrop of an Odeon cinema, once common throughout the country in competition with the Gaumont group, RT4580 is nearly halfway through its stay at Leyton garage. The date is 3rd August and as the bus travels to Finsbury Park Station on Route 106 the weather conditions appear perfect. (A.B.Cross)

The penultimate RTL, 1630, entered revenue service in April of the year under review from Middle Row garage. Delivered new to London Transport in November 1954 it was immediately put into store, initially at Reigate before being moved to Shepherds Bush and then Clapham garages. Its period of idleness ending in its last move to Garston where it was prepared for service. It is seen on a route diversion heading into Northumberland Avenue to reach the Victoria Embankment one Sunday in March when a huge anti-apartheid rally was held in Trafalgar Square. South Africa House had been cordoned off, although traffic appears to have been allowed to pass in front, and Duncannon Street and the Strand were closed. (M.Dryhurst)

An interesting selection of parked cars can be seen in this picture with, to the left, a post-war Standard 8 and to the right an Austin 12/16 with an Austin 10 behind. Centrepiece is RT963 which calls in at Hertford Bus Station on its way from Sele Farm Estate to Enfield on Route 310. At its January 1960 overhaul a Weymann non-roof box body was substituted for the one currently carried and the bus continued in service until July 1972. (A.R.Packer)

RF492 had initially entered service in March 1953 being garaged at Sidcup. It would eventually be withdrawn from passenger use after the last full day of services by the Central Area variety of the class on 30th March 1979. Having received an overhaul in August 1957 it re-entered service garaged at Dalston and is caught by the camera on the stand at Bromley by Bow while working Route 208. (A.Mortimer)

Traversing the main road through Oxted, RLH18 continues its journey to Bromley North Station on Route 410. The cast iron road sign beneath the ageing trees directs road users to either the local railway station or to Godstone some two miles distant in the direction from which the bus has travelled. (A.R.Packer)

Sometime during September GS44 with running plates HG22 waits in Hertford Bus Station in readiness for the Saturday additional service at 13.03 to Gilston. Eventually when the bus finished its passenger use at this garage in October 1960 it spent a few weeks on staff bus duties at Abbey Wood and North Street, Romford before returning to normal work at Epping garage. Later service at Dorking was followed by a return visit to Hertford. Final withdrawal came in August 1966. (A.R.Packer)

With the Christmas festivities now over and the New Year celebrations still to follow, Chelsham's RF186 drops off passengers in the deserted Watford town centre on Sunday 28th December. Route 707 ran between Aylesbury and Oxted using the same roads as the 706 service until at the southern end of the routes at Botley Hill, the 707 continued on the B269 road for Oxted while 706 used the B2024 to reach its destination of Westerham. Joined with the 708 Hemel Hempstead to East Grinstead route the three Green Lines contrived to give a daily 15 minute service between Two Waters and South Croydon. (A.R.Packer)

Initially entering the preservation movement in November 1977, RF421 is currently in the custody of John Stanley of Gravesend. The bus had entered service as a Central Area 2RF2 carrying body number 7939 in January 1953 and is seen here on Route 237at Hounslow Bus Station, having received an overhaul in the previous December, when it re-emerged from works with body number 7998. After two further body changes it gained body number 8793 at its last overhaul in March 1973. This was originally a Country Area bus repainted red in May 1969 and today it still carries this red livery. (P.Gomm collection)

At Ilford on 24th December Seven Kings garaged RT2370 heads several identical looking buses occupying the stand in York Road. The lead bus is about to work Route 150 to Chigwell Row, Maypole Inn. Up until the previous month RT2370 had been garaged at Holloway but with the large programme of vehicle movements on the night of 25th/26th November it moved across to its present home assisting in the complete withdrawal of the RTL class of bus from AP. (A.R.Packer)

Ex-B19 has worn the Brighton, Hove and District red and cream livery since acquisition in May 1953. The original Duple body was removed and scrapped in December 1954 being replaced with this fine new Eastern Coachworks product. It carries fleet number 5998 in this view taken on 12th April. Renumbered 998 in April 1960 it continued in service until August 1965 and was sold on in October of that year. (A.R.Packer)

Route 39 was extended to Waterloo from Victoria to serve St.Thomas' Hospital on Sunday afternoons and evenings and consequently renumbered 39A on 12th January of the year under review. Here Battersea's RTW324 is seen at the Waterloo terminus before departure back to Southfields Station. The fact that it carries running number B10 proves the photograph to be taken before 30th April when the route's allocation was reduced to six. The service proved greatly underused and was withdrawn in the same year, operating for the last time on 23rd November. (J.A.S. Hambley collection)

Trade plate 015GH is carried by one of the two Routemaster mobile test rigs used to shadow buses in normal service thereby gaining experience in the characteristics of the new concept. Turning many heads, these two unusual vehicles presented the casual observer with the question 'What were they?'. Basically assembled using two full length welded structures to which the A and B frames were attached they had a flat lorry type platform body mounted with a front cab and observation saloon. The weight of a fully laden bus was simulated using sandbags. In September this particular unit shadows a Route 11 bus and is seen negotiating the Buckingham Palace Road/Ebury Bridge Road junction. (Dave Berwick)

Former RT1463 was purchased by the Dundee Corporation Transport Department via Bird's Commercial Motors of Stratford upon Avon in August 1956. It is seen in Dundee town centre sometime during September of the year under review while in use on Route 19 as it rides the stone setts and crosses the disused rails of the tramway system, which were last used in 1956. (R.Hobbs)

With the first phase of the new face of Luton, in the shape of the enhanced wing to the existing education buildings now proudly completed, a clear unobstructed wide pavement is enjoyed by the queue of waiting travellers. At this long standing terminal point in Park Street RF617 of Hitchin garage waits in the sunshine for some human contact before departure to its home town by way of the various villages of north Hertfordshire served by Route 364. (Photobus)

The railway bridge over Wells Terrace at Finsbury Park carried lines into the coal yard to the north of the road. Beneath it RF454 and another sister bus wait their respective departure times on the busy 212 route to Muswell Hill, nowadays numbered W7. During its life with London Transport five different bodies were carried by the chassis of this RF commencing with 7972 in February 1953 when it first entered service. Since July 1957 7978 has been fitted while in later years 7935, then 7907 and finally 7914 all served their time in maintaining the fleet number in passenger use until withdrawn in April 1976. (A.R.Packer)

After nearly four years in storage at Loughton garage since delivery, RT4762 entered service operating out of Leatherhead in April of the year under review. It is seen here at Epsom Station on a 406 or 406A journey, depending on which number blind you consult, although since it is only travelling as far as the Downs it is immaterial. (A.Mortimer)

The lowest numbered post-war RT carried fleet number RT152 and, still fitted with its original Park Royal body numbered 1401, it now enjoys further passenger use with the Ayrshire Bus Owners' Consortium. Pictured at the Ardrossan terminal, on 31st July in the predominantly blue A1 Services livery it carries the quaint destination of Stevenston, Pillar Box, which has been referred to before in this series of books. The year under review witnessed the first sales of standard post-war examples of the RT class together with members of the RTL class and after nearly eleven years service in the capital this bus was included in the February sales, being quickly recognised as a bargain by its new owners. (A.R.Packer)

The date is 20th July and at Hemel Hempstead bus station RF599 awaits departure time on Route 322 to Watford Junction. The bus station building is completed with a fine roof mounted London Transport sign, although the 'King Harry' public house has yet to appear. The bus was converted to one-man operation in October of the year under review. (J.C.Gillham)

RT912 has worn Country Area livery since July 1956 when it re-entered service after its second overhaul, having previously been in the central red colour scheme, firstly at Hounslow and subsequently at Peckham and New Cross garages. It is seen in Clarendon Road, Watford on 28th December as it continues in service to Leavesden, Ganders Ash on Route 306 and working from Watford High Street garage. Local advertising for the current panto-mime production 'Robinson Crusoe' at the Watford Palace Theatre is carried on the front panels and the theatre itself can be seen to the left of the picture. (A.R.Packer)

RT1051 hopefully will attract some patronage before a journey from Kingston railway station to Tadworth by way of the Monday-Friday peak hour express version of Route 406A. 'Express' was the London Transport term for what were essentially limited stop journeys. This bus will take 38 minutes to reach Tadworth while the normal 406A lurking in the left hand corner of the picture will take 50 minutes over the trip. (Photobus)

At the Oxford Road, Putney terminus of Route 14 RTW417's driver, hands clamped firmly on the steering wheel in the optimum 10 to 2 driving position, looks on as his conductor strides away from an inspector. Perhaps agreement has just been reached on the South Kensington Station turn as shown on the destination blind. The date is 22nd November and the trees in the background, having shed their leaves sometime previously, will not add any beauty to the drab surroundings until the following spring. The bus carries F running plates but with the closure of Putney Bridge garage after the 25th of the month it would transfer to the Chelverton Road establishment from where most of the closed garage's concentration of the class would henceforth operate. (A.R.Packer)

Crew operated RF558 is soon to depart from Redhill for the Monotype Works at Salfords by way of Route 440 on 20th September. Only this one route served the works which was situated halfway between the town and Horley, just off the main A23 down the beautifully named Honeycrock Lane. This RF had been overhauled in January of the year under review, re-entering service at St.Albans garage and after several transfers it settled down at Reigate in June. Converted to one person operation in February 1959, the bus was transferred to East Grinstead in May of that same year. (A.R.Packer)

An offside view of ex-STD72, then in the ownership of Hutfields Coaches, appeared in the 1957 book of this series. In February of the year under review L.E.A.Coaches of Coventry acquired the bus and after only two months it passed on to its last documented owner, Young's International Coaches Ltd. of Grays. It is seen in the picture above parked at Thundersley in Essex on 7th April still basically in the Hutfields livery. Later in the year the lower picture finds it in Eastwoodbury Crescent at Southend-on-Sea in a new very anonymous paint scheme. (F.Church (above), B.Pask (below))

At Raynes Park some particularly attractive railings adorn the first floor level above the shops while RT3020 with its classic appearance occupies the immediate roadway. The following bus, RTL877, is destined for Worcester Park Station on route 189A. This dates the picture to between 20th August and 25th November which was the period during which the 189A had a Monday to Friday peak hour extension to this point. (Photobus)

RT1661 with running plates MA1 is seen en-route for High Wycombe LT Garage while in service on Route 362, having stopped at Chesham sometime in December. Prior to 14th May the 362 route had worked via Anne's Corner at Amersham but was then re-routed direct via Chesham Road thereby removing the 362A variation. A number of RTs returned to service after overhaul in September 1957 having received green livery in lieu of Central Area red and included this example. A very rare Triumph Mayflower manufactured between 1949 and 1953 has caused the bus to stop at an angle and it is interesting to note that the saloon car carries a 1954 registration. (A.R.Packer)

RFW11 takes a well-earned rest from its latest private hire venture at Hampton Court railway station. In the fashion of the period, all unnecessary polished aluminium trim to the lower edge of the bodywork, rear wheels and chrome front wheel fittings have been painted in line with the main bodywork colour, which diminished the eye-catching appeal of these otherwise luxury coaches. (M.Dryhurst)

Elsewhere in this book you will find a picture of an Upton Park RT working Route 145. This garage had an allocation of both the AECs and Leylands from 1954, the numbers fluctuating from time to time. After the November 1958 reductions however the RTLs departed leaving only the RTW Leylands which the garage used on the 15 route. RTL1621, which had first entered service in March of the year now under review, moved on to West Green garage with the November changes. It is working one of the special journeys on the 145 to Dagenham Dock and is passing some of the redevelopment taking place in Ilford. (A.R.Packer)

Originally a private hire coach, RF18 was converted for use as a Green Line coach in May 1956 being allocated to Northfleet five months later. By 1958 it had found its way to Hertford and here is working the Monday to Friday daytime short section of Route 372, which provided a town service in Welwyn Garden City between Great Ganett and Lemsford Lane. This rather bleak 'bus station' at Welwyn Garden City Station is now covered by the Howard Shopping Centre. The 372 route was part of a complete reorganisation of the Hertford routes on 22nd July when it was extended beyond Hertford to Coopersale Street, replacing the 399 and at the same time was fully converted to one-man-operation, making RF18's use as a bus redundant, at least on this route. In the same re-shuffle most of these short workings were removed from the timetable. (P.J.Malsher)

RT185 now carries its final body, number 1557, having been outshopped from overhaul in March of the previous year. Here at Wembley Empire Pool sometime in the same month of the year now under review it waits a further trip on Route 92. A Renault 4CV developed during World War II and the mainstay of Renault production for many post-war years is seen on the left of the picture, the driver having ignored the 'no parking' sign. (A.R.Packer)

The experimental department at Chiswick Works used RT3995 from March 1951 through to November 1965 when it was moved to Catford after completing its years of experimentation. The bus had entered service with five others at Leyton garage in December 1950, unsuspecting that three months later it would cease its revenue earning service with London Transport for so long. In this view, taken beside the experimental shop, which was out of bounds to non-authorised persons, the bus is clearly seen with some investigation in progress with cable leading from the wheels to the interior via opening windows. Eventually sold in September 1966 it still carried the combination of chassis and Weymann bodywork as first delivered. (J.A.S. Hambley collection)

A different approach to displaying the route number was taken with the non-roof box variety RTs acquired by Bradford Corporation. The route number was shown in a small section of the old via points box in order to give a symmetrical appearance. Here, standing in the city centre on 10th August, ex-RT156 now carrying fleet number 402 below the driver's windscreen, waits departure on a journey to Little Horton via Heaton, which places lie to the north west of the city. (A.R.Packer)

This is not a London Transport service or vehicle but is an example of frustration caused by LT's inadequacies in 1958. In October the Finchley Liberal Party were so incensed by the poor service given to Hampstead Garden Suburb by the 102 bus route that they provided a free service for commuters between Golders Green and East Finchley. Coaches were hired from Finchley Coaches and RPG491, a full fronted Dennis, turns out of The Bishop's Avenue on to Lyttelton Way on the service. (D.W.K.Jones)

GS 61, 63, 68, 70 and 72 ventured to the seaside town of Great Yarmouth on loan for less than a year and GS63 is pictured here with the Britannia Pier as a backdrop. It is en-route for Cobholm by way of route 6 which will take it via the Sea Front and Town Centre. Upon their return in July 1959 all five buses were initially put into store in the basement at Gillingham Street garage, Victoria. Although two did see further service with LT, this example did not and it was later moved to Grays and then London Road, Romford in permanent unlicensed condition. Eventually it found a buyer in May 1961 from which point it was taken on board as a preservation project although it now carries the identification of GS61! (J.A.S. Hambley collection)

On 28th December GS67 awaits departure on the short journey from the Rickmansworth car park stand on the By-Pass to Loudwater Village on Route 336A. A reasonable load of passengers has boarded this essentially 'community' bus service. The long shadows and leafless trees and shrubbery suggest a cold crisp winter's day. Many years later this bus saw passenger service as one of the Surrey Hills leisure buses. (A.R.Packer)

The Sunday hospital route 400, which only ran between June and October of the year under review, was maintained by one GS bus operated by Chelsham garage. On this particular journey GS38 is seen complete with an inspector, possibly navigating its journey to Warlingham Park Hospital which started at New Addington, Parkway and encountered some fairly remote country lanes en route. (Ron Wellings)

Two gentlemen consult the times of first and last buses fixed to the bus stop in Praed Street for routes 7,15 and 23A while RTW119 pauses on its journey to East Ham, White Horse. Cold November weather prevailing, the all Leyland product, last overhauled in February 1957, looks decidedly in need of a visit through the washing facilities at Upton Park garage. (A.R.Packer)

ST587 is seen in Colston Avenue, Bristol sometime during the latter part of its loan to Bristol Tramways during the war years. Twelve of the ST class made the journey from London to Bristol in December 1942 but it was not until January 1944 that local fleet numbers were applied to the vehicles. The fleet number 3703 can just be made out below the rear platform window. Someone has also repositioned the registration plate, presumably because the London practice of putting it inside the platform was not considered sufficiently prominent in Bristol. All the twelve STs returned to London in February 1946 and resumed passenger service for varied periods, this one lasting until October 1949 when it ended its days at Holloway. (J.A.S.Hambley collection)

GX131, a Leyland TD1 with petrol engine and operator built bodywork entered service in 1932 with Birch Brothers Ltd. It was re-engined with a diesel unit in June 1933 and then acquired by LPTB on 21st February 1934 together with other Birch vehicles. Numbered TD85 it survived until August 1939 when it was acquired by Canvey and District Motor Services through the Leeds dealer, W.North. Canvey numbered it 25 and rebuilt it with an AEC 7.7 litre oil engine together with appropriate radiator. Here it is seen during the war years on the long standing service 3 between South Benfleet and Southend. The conductor stands beside a typical pre-war bus stop of the area and the military truck adds to the period atmosphere. (Omnibus Society)

On 1st September 1942 ST249 is seen departing from the West Yorkshire Road Car Company bus station in Vicar Lane, Leeds for a journey to Harrogate. Eight STs were loaned to this operator from 1st August 1942 returning to London in September 1944 whereupon they immediately re-entered service. Anti-blast netting has disappeared from some windows and paper stickers now display route details but in other respects the bus is in the condition in which it had recently left London. (J.A.S.Hambley collection)

Country Area bus route 369 was born out of the World War II conflict when Green Line routes were suspended from 1st September 1939. A partial resumption of these services commenced on 1st November although by then a number of new bus routes had been introduced to cover stretches of road left unserved by the initial withdrawals. To cover the absence of service between St.Albans and Dunstable, previously provided by Green Line H2, the 369 started operation on 25th September. St.Albans' STL2008 has arrived at Dunstable Square with silver painted roof, white tipped mudguards, restricted side and headlights and anti-blast netting applied to the lower saloon windows only. Having been transferred from Victoria garage on 25th June 1941, repaint from red to green for this vehicle did not occur until April 1945. By that time the silver roof would have been long gone and it is surprising that it still remains at the time this picture was taken. (Omnibus Society)

In its first years of existence T630 had a varied career starting with Green Line duties from Staines in August 1938. Converted to an ambulance at the outbreak of World War II it was re-converted for passenger use during November 1939. In January 1943, along with other members of the class, it was lent to the American Red Cross who had fifty-five vehicles converted to 'Clubmobiles'. Fitted with two beds for the resident assistants, known as 'Doughgirls', and equipped with all the paraphernalia required for their new role as canteens, they saw service at airfields and camps with concentrations of American forces throughout the British Isles. Returned to LPTB in November 1945 this coach resumed Green Line duties in May 1946 operating from Addlestone garage. (Fox Photos)

— 1948 —

In central London an enquiring traveller converses with the conductor of T484 while the driver looks on anxiously wishing to get on with the journey to Woking on Route 717. Having endured the indignity of being equipped as a public ambulance capable of carrying 8 to 10 stretchers for much of the war years, the coach's return to service in March 1946 was part of the resumption of Green Line services at that time. Eventually in April 1953 the vehicle would further its chequered career, which had commenced in May 1938, by being exported to Yugoslavia. (R.Wellings)

T555 with running plates HG40 waits departure from Hertford bus station for a journey on Route 390 to Stevenage via Stapleford and Watton-at-Stone with a detour up to Aston thrown in. The smoke escaping from the chimney stack has nothing to do with the 10T10 although it does appear as if it were part of the coach's ventilating system. (D.A.Thompson)

A very wet St.Mary's Square, Hitchin provides the layover point for Hatfield garaged STL980 between its journeys on Route 303. This bus was one of the first series of Country Area normal height front entrance STLs which entered service over a six month period during 1935 fitted with LPTB bodywork. Small modifications since its initial entry into service include the added nearside driver's mirror, sidelights moved from the corners between decks and an added route stencil holder placed at the top of the window to the saloon entrance. The conductor poses in the entrance displaying the standard equipment of his trade in 1948. (D.A.Thompson)

LT391 set up ready for its next journey to Victoria on Route 38 has been backed on to the stand at the Royal Forest Hotel, Chingford. Originally entering service in March 1931 fitted with a Strachan built body incorporating a one piece route box it is now in its final form with an LT5/7 type of body built by LGOC having a full complement of blind boxes. Withdrawn from service in November 1949 it made a last journey to Daniels of Rainham during the same month. Behind the LT is one of the trailer canteens which was parked, somewhat unusually, on private property at this site. (D.A.Thompson)

The conductor rings the driver off at the start of another 310 journey from Cecil Road, Enfield to Hertford while dad upstairs enjoys his pipe and keeps a watchful eye on his young charge. ST1060 had but a few more weeks to run before the body would be separated from the chassis and any useful parts removed for further use in maintaining other buses in a serviceable condition, ending nineteen years of public service. (D.A.Thompson)

In the wartime supplement to this book an STL is seen at the Dunstable terminus of Route 369. Here, a few years later, an older bus in the form of ST1120 is found at the other end of the route in St.Peters Street, St.Albans loading for departure to Dunstable. Now nearing the end of its many years of operational service, it had originally entered service in May 1930 owned by the LGOC but operating for East Surrey Traction Company as their fleet number 243. Withdrawn from service in October 1949 with its distinctive Ransomes, Sims and Jefferies body it was scrapped soon afterwards. (R.Wellings)

Parked at Chertsey Station LT1015 waits before returning to Hounslow on Route 237 during its stay at Hounslow garage. The single deck representatives of the class rebuilt by Marshalls of Cambridge were all returned to London in the post-war colour scheme of red and cream with this example having received attention during the period July to December 1948. A further four years passenger use culminated in it being withdrawn soon after transfer to Sutton garage, having completed twenty-two years service within the capital. (R.Wellings)

In 1949 former staff canteen 38H (previously No.10 and prior to that NS2169) was a familiar sight to travellers between North Cheam and Morden, parked as it was at Sullin's Farm, Ridge Road just off Stonecot Hill. First entering service at Plumstead garage during the second half of 1926, the bus was initially fitted with solid tyres and carried an LGOC built body. The last examples of the class operated by LPTB in passenger service ran on the night of 30th November 1937 with plans having been made for twenty-four to be converted for service vehicle duties. The Tramway Department had nine while three were converted to tree lopper use and twelve were converted as mobile staff canteens. Disposed of in November 1948 to Lammas Motors of south west London this old timer ended up amid the haystacks and farm implements. (A.M.Wright)

Newly overhauled LT1101 re-entered service during the summer of 1949 and is seen helping out at Victoria Station on Route 10 during its short stay at Leyton. Further use at Kingston and Elmers End ended with withdrawal from service in October 1950 and sale to Daniels the dealer of Rainham in Essex. This particular 'scooter' was not one of those converted to diesel. (D.A.Jones)

During its last year in the ownership of the Executive, T251 is seen carrying makeshift route details for its use on Route 53 from Plumstead Common to East Greenwich. The blind box originally consisted of a two strip arrangement for its Green Line use when the coach first entered service in January 1931. Relegated to bus duties in March 1938 the box was rebuilt to accommodate a larger display area. Disposed of in June 1949, the vehicle found further use with independent operators until finally scrapped by Deacon, a dealer of Dorchester in Oxfordshire (not the more well known Dorset town) in November 1951. (J.A.S.Hambley collection)

ST274 spent the last few months of its service in the capital garaged at Tottenham and is seen parked at Stoke Newington while waiting for its next trip to Waterloo on Route 67. For just over a year during the war it operated on producer gas, which was its only deviation from an otherwise routine life which lasted from August 1930 until withdrawal in May 1949. The J.Arthur Rank film 'The Blue Lagoon' is advertised on the side while some sort of escape from the austerity of the post-war years is offered by the Daily Mail Ideal Home Exhibition which ran from 1st to 26th March of this particular year. (D.A.Thompson)

Still in pristine new condition, Muswell Hill's TD81 stands at Arnos Grove Station before departure on Route 251 to Burnt Oak, Edgware Road having entered service during April 1949. One hundred of these Mann Egerton bodied Leyland PS1 buses were delivered over a thirteen month period commencing 1948 to replace Ts and single deck LTs on a variety of routes. Muswell Hill had received the original thirty-one Weymann bodied examples in 1947 and then two years later they were given nine of the Mann Egerton variety to convert the rather rural 251 route, although they soon became intermixed with the older batch. (D.A.Thompson)

— 1950 —

LT1112 climbing Muswell Hill on Route 212 passes the junction of Springfield Avenue with a standing load and finds the gradient eases a little before the final 1 in 7 assault past the Ritz Cinema to its terminus at Muswell Hill Broadway. Now fitted with a diesel engine it doubtless finds the task a little easier than it would in its petrol days before February 1950. My colleague David Ruddom tells me this is the very spot at which he spent many a happy half hour in the peak watching the performance of the 'scooters' sometimes accompanied by jets of steam from the radiators. New in June 1931, this example was finally sold to a dealer in Newport called Morgan in August 1953. (R.Wellings)

RTW247 during its first few months of operation is seen on route 114 as it journeys to Edgware L.T.Station. On the extreme right of the picture is one of a large number of Police Public Call Boxes, familiar to devotees of 'Doctor Who'. A first aid box is available in the box and the blue light above the roof will flash when the police station wants to contact the local beat 'Bobby'. Kerbstones around the road junction are still painted in blackout fashion while one of the attractive pre-war bus shelters completes an interesting picture thought to have been taken at the junction of Marsh Lane and Whitchurch Lane. (R.Wellings)

At Victoria station forecourt STD105 in its last full year of passenger operation waits to journey to Ladbroke Grove on the 52. The utility bodied Leyland TD7 chassis spent its entire revenue earning career from July 1942 through to February 1951 garaged at Victoria. No doubt this driver cursed the allocation of this sluggish beast to his duty, particularly as a gleaming Willesden RT waits behind ready to catch him up in no time. In the next bay Cricklewood garaged SRT50 waits to depart for Sudbury Town on Route 16. This combination of RT type bodywork mounted on the chassis of ex-STL2617 initially took to the road as a learner vehicle in June 1949. (J.A.S.Hambley collection)

Front entrance STL1026 is in use at Slough on Windsor's Route 446 displaying the unusual blind arrangement used on this group of routes. With restricted blinds still the norm, the information as to the direction the bus would take to reach Farnham Road was shown in the number blind box. When full blind displays were re-introduced the destination blind was used for this purpose. (R.Wellings)

T250 as an 11T11 stands outside the original Amersham & District Motor Bus & Haulage Co.Ltd. premises together with another of the type and a Leyland Cub. The route blind is wound for the 394C service which was the number used for garage journeys to and from Hyde Heath between 1st July 1942 and 13th May 1958. All thirty-one of this type of bus, which carried Weymann built bodies from scrapped Reliance chassis, entered service in the Country Area. During their period of operation twenty-two received Central Area livery at varying dates, including this example. This one is unique however in that its operation as a red bus only lasted between May 1942 and October 1943 and it became the only one to revert back to its original colours. (J.G.S.Smith collection)

STL2656 withdrawn from service and immediately disposed of to Daniels of Rainham in February 1950 passed on to the Denver Chemical Company after having been cut down to perform as a lorry. New legal lettering together with an AEC triangle at the top of the radiator have replaced that carried previously and the vehicle looks very business like. (D.A.Jones)

KNO608 carrying Eastern National fleet number 3905 is a Bristol L5G with ECW 35 seat rear entrance body which had been transferred to London Transport with the services in the Grays and Tilbury area on 30th September 1951. Standing outside the Queens Hotel in Grays during November the bus is working Route 85 which had run between here and Woodside Estate since 11th May 1947. This route would be linked in due course with the London Transport Route 370A to form new routes 328 and 328A. The GY18 running plates, which are painted red to indicate operation from Argent Street, the former ENOC depot, hardly show against the background of Tilling green. (D.F.Parker)

Before the arrival of the first batch of the RLH class in 1950 the lowbridge fleet of London Transport had consisted of a small number of different types. There were seven Short and one Strachan bodied STs, twelve 'Godstone' STLs, twenty further STLs which had received austerity wartime built bodies in place of those carried earlier and ten utility D class. ST140, one of the oldest with the double sunken gangway upper deck layout, journeys to Ottershaw on Route 461A sometime during its last full year of operation. (LCC Tramways Trust collection)

Most of the bodywork of ST314 had been removed and scrapped in May 1948 with the chassis and front portion of its lower deck serving as a towing vehicle within the grounds of Chiswick Works through to July 1954. Looking very dejected and unkempt, it stands alongside a CR and a 4Q4 in various states of disrepair. (LCC Tramways Trust collection)

T466 departs Epping garage to take up duty for a journey to Windsor on Green Line Route 718 while C65 arrives, having completed a journey on Route 381. Both vehicles would be withdrawn from service in 1953 with no further history being recorded for the T after initial disposal to W.North, the Leeds dealer. The C passed through the hands of the same dealer and was exported to Ceylon in January 1954, being identified later carrying local registration number IC2484. (LCC Tramways Trust collection)

T454 is seen at South Park, 'Holmesdale', working the Reigate to Redhill service 430. It still carries Green Line livery from its previous duties and this colour scheme had been maintained at its last overhaul in July 1951. Displaced from coach work at the time its previous garage, Crawley, received a small batch of new RFs in December 1951, it was temporarily used at Reigate before transfer to the Central Area in July 1952 for bus duties, first at Kingston then Croydon and back to Kingston again before withdrawal. (R.Hobbs)

STL1642, a 4/9STL11, finished its operational career with London Transport in September 1952 and for a few months had enjoyed service fitted again with a full complement of blinds. It is seen departing Southall garage with destination set for a short journey to Park Royal Station emphasised by the word 'only'. Subsequently the bus spent a further period as a training vehicle at Norbiton and Dalston garages and was finally disposed of to W.North, the Leeds dealer, in April 1955. (J.A.S.Hambley collection)

This corner of Park Square, Luton with the junction of Church Street has completely changed with the Luton University and Arndale Shopping Centre now occupying the background. STL2147, last overhauled in July 1951, had started life as a red liveried 4/9STL15 but its body was removed in May 1949 and scrapped, being replaced by this green liveried STL16 variety previously mounted on the chassis of STL2558. Having arrived at the setting down point the bus will move to the stand situated across the road once the pedestrian with hands in pockets gets out of the way. Transferred to Dartford three months before withdrawal, most of its use in the Country Area was spent in and around Luton. (R.Wellings)

Hertford garage suddenly received an influx of TF vehicles in February 1952, which had been displaced at Dorking with the delivery of new RF coaches. The former coaches worked on most of Hertford's single deck routes. TF23 is seen opposite Potters Bar garage en-route for New Barnet Station on Route 342 and this vehicle survived until its withdrawal in June 1953 when it passed to W.North Ltd. (R.Wellings)

Almost every London Transport number-crunching schoolboy's dream appears to have been realised for this group venturing inside Reigate garage. The two centrally parked Cubs can be identified as CR33 and CR40 while one of the Inter Station Cubs together with an STL stand further within the premises. This particular view evokes nostalgia in the author, who tried unsuccessfully on a number of occasions to penetrate the depths of this particular garage all those years ago. (R.Hobbs)

Dereliction within the premises of Vass at Ampthill in Bedfordshire continues to this day but for a particular period it was a poignant scene for the London bus enthusiast as this view shows. The line up of unwanted vehicles from left to right is T424, G149 and CR30, the latter of which disappeared the following year. T424 was finally scrapped in 1958 while the Guy Arab was reduced to scrap metal in 1966 after being used as a store shed. (J.H.Price)

Sunday excursions to a variety of destinations made enjoyable family days out before the advent of the private car. A large number of buses, having reached their destination of London Airport, now wait the return journeys with tired but hopefully satisfied passengers. The front row from left to right consists of RT2691, STD23, RTL847 and RTL834 on Excursions 37, 33, 31 and another 31 originating from Palmers Green, Enfield and Clapham respectively. (R.Wellings)

First entering service in June 1934, STL441 now carries body number 14503, which was the fourth body to be fitted to the chassis and it is this combination which can still be viewed at Cobham, the home of the London Bus Preservation Trust. On 16th April 1952, with AK12 running plates, it is seen on its way from Clapham Common to Raynes Park on Route 118 while members of the locally ubiquitous D class make an interesting background at Morden Underground station. Withdrawn from service in September 1952, the STL was later put on display within the Netherlands Auto Museum ensuring its continued preservation and eventual return to this country. (A.B.Cross)

The PSV Circle documents STL1428 as being disposed of to Daniels of Rainham for scrap in December 1949 but here it is seen very much alive and in use as some sort of showman's transport at a fair in Mitcham in April 1952. With its top deck above the lower window line removed, the familiar shape and lines of the remains of its LPTB built STL11 body are clearly evident. (J.A.S.Hambley collection)

In what appears to be the depths of the Hertfordshire countryside but is now well within the Hemel Hempstead New Town, T786 journeys to Clarendon Corner, Watford on the 320 route. Overhauled in June 1951, the latest green and cream livery is carried in place of the original dark green and white which had been worn by all thirty of the Mann Egerton bodied AEC Regals. Operated by Two Waters garage since new in July 1948, a move to the newly opened Garston garage occurred on 18th June 1952, the 320 route seen here being withdrawn a week earlier on the 10th. (R.Wellings)

Temporary refuge is provided at Dover Docks in July 1953 for, from left to right, T276 and T261 before their turn comes to be shipped to the continent. Just where they ended up is one of life's mysteries but they had been disposed of by the Executive to the Benhill Machinery and Equipment Company of London W1 earlier in the year. Both buses are of the 11T11 classification, a combination of AEC Regal chassis originally fitted with coach type bodies which were replaced by these Weymann bus examples, which had already been used to re-body AEC Reliances. (J.A.S.Hambley collection)

Standing in Crawley old town, STL1011 now carries rear entrance bodywork in lieu of the front entrance STL6 example fitted when new in May 1935. It now bears an STL14 body numbered 16994 which it retained until scrapped by W.North, the Leeds dealer in June 1955. With CY14 running plates, it waits departure on the 483 New Town route to Northgate introduced on 6th May 1953. (D.F.Parker)

The full blind display had returned to the capital in 1950 on newly delivered vehicles. With the STL class only one solitary example had been unmasked during 1951, although many appeared in the following July. STL1677, in use on Route 402, carries a 'lazy' Sevenoaks & Dunton Green' destination which is at least enhanced by the comprehensive via point display. (D.F.Parker)

The special blind display and slipboard confirm the use of RT352 on the special Coronation Day service on the northern end of the fragmented Route 59 which operated between West Hampstead Station and Baker Street Station, where this picture is taken. Fourteen RT class buses were employed on this service from Cricklewood garage while thirty-one similar vehicles from Croydon and Thornton Heath provided a service at the southern end from Lambeth North Station to Chipstead Valley. (D.A.Jones)

The Park Royal body number 17591 carried by STL2170 when it entered service in September 1937 had been replaced by identical 17549 at the time of its May 1939 overhaul. This in turn had given way to LPTB built body 103 in May 1949 when the chassis to which it had been mounted was required for SRT conversion. In November 1951 it was repainted into Country Area livery and operated by Grays, London Road Romford and Windsor before transfer to St.Albans around Christmas 1952. Now fitted with a full blind display the bus journeys to Fleetville on the circular service 354 in winter sunshine. (R.Wellings)

STL1218 with its unique BXB letter registration is fitted with one of the last three bodies classified STL12 used in revenue service, all of which ended their passenger service while garaged at Upton Park. Prior to transfer there it is seen operating from Hornchurch garage in Romford on Route 165 to Rainham War Memorial with full blind display. (D.F.Parker)

Normally a resident of Dunton Green garage, STL1940 has been drafted in to help move the racing enthusiasts to and from Epsom Downs. It is seen here at the racecourse with STL1677 next in line, both waiting their turn to be 'filled up' in an organised fashion for the run down to Epsom Station on Route 406F. Both bodies are of the STL14 classification, the first roofbox variant, although close examination reveal slight differences received over roughly seventeen years service. (D.F.Parker)

After long term storage at Grays, STL2348 has returned to service at Staines for a short while before transfer to Dunton Green for a few final months of passenger use and withdrawal in October 1953. One of the last green and cream liveried STLs to be operated in passenger service, it stands in the Kingston railway station terminus before departure on a race day extra on Route 406 to Epsom Downs. (D.F.Parker)

TD33 is parked in South Street, Romford sometime during April 1953 with the classic frontage of an ABC cinema behind. The route blind, with a little adjustment, would show the two termini of Romford Station and Romford, Birch Road used by Route 252 at the time. At the beginning of 1958 the route would be extended north to Collier Row and in November of that year south to South Hornchurch but for the moment the nine minute shuttle was all that was required of the Leyland single decker. The bus looks a little tired and worn and would receive its second overhaul a year later, returning to Hornchurch to continue an association which had started in October 1948. (D.F.Parker)

In later years the Epsom race meetings provided less of interest in terms of variety of vehicles which operated the special service between Morden Station and the racecourse. However, in 1953 STD130 with Leyton running plates leads a similar vehicle on to the Downs adding a little relief from the now commonplace RTs and RTLs. (D.F.Parker)

Christmas 1953 witnessed Dunton Green's STL670 pressed into Green Line relief duties on Route 704. Driver and inspector compare notes before departure from Eccleston Bridge, Victoria with an impressive front full blind display. The STL5 body built by LPTB and numbered 14583 was one of the small number of the type which saw service through to the final year of pre-war STL operation. (D.F.Parker)

Green Line T460 entered service in February 1938 from Windsor garage. Converted to a public ambulance this vehicle was re-converted for passenger use early in the war. However in November 1942 it was sent to the O.C.Motor Base of the U.S.Forces in England at Ashchurch, Gloucestershire for use by the U.S.Army. In May 1946 the coach returned to passenger use, not with London Transport but with D.J.Davies of Merthyr Tydfil re-registered HB6138. After later use with Neath & Cardiff Luxury Coaches, the mark of whose emblem can just be made out between saloon door and rear wheel arch, it managed a credible nine years use as a caravan. Parked on wasteland, the intriguing rolling stock in the background might eventually help in identifying the location. (LCC Tramways Trust collection)

APPENDIX I

London Transport Central and Country Area Bus Garages

A	Sutton	K	Kingston
AB	Twickenham	L	Loughton
AC	Willesden	LH*	Leatherhead
AD	Palmers Green	LS*	Luton
AE	Hendon	M	Mortlake
AF	Chelverton Road, Putney	MA*	Amersham
AK	Streatham	MH	Muswell Hill
AL	Merton	N	Norwood
AM	Plumstead	NB	Norbiton
AP	Seven Kings	NF*	Northfleet
AR	Tottenham	NS	North Street, Romford
AV	Hounslow	NX	New Cross
AW	Abbey Wood	ON	Alperton
B	Battersea	P	Old Kent Road
BK	Barking	PB	Potters Bar
BN	Brixton	PM	Peckham
C	Athol Street, Poplar	Q	Camberwell
CA	Clapham	R	Riverside
CF	Chalk Farm	RD	Hornchurch
CL	Clay Hall	RE*	London Road, Romford
CM*	Chelsham	RG*	Reigate
CS	Chiswick (non-operational)	RL	Rye Lane
CY*	Crawley	S	Shepherds Bush
D	Dalston	SA*	St.Albans
DG*	Dunton Green	SJ*	Swanley Junction
DS*	Dorking	SP	Sidcup
DT*	Dartford	ST*	Staines
E	Enfield	SV*	Stevenage
ED	Elmers End	SW	Stockwell
EG*	East Grinstead	T	Leyton
EP*	Epping	TB	Bromley
EW	Edgware	TC	Croydon
F	Putney Bridge	TG*	Tring
G	Forest Gate	TH	Thornton Heath
GD*	Godstone	TL	Catford
GF*	Guildford	TW*	Tunbridge Wells
GM	Gillingham Street, Victoria	U	Upton Park
GR*	Garston	UX	Uxbridge
GY*	Grays	V	Turnham Green
H	Hackney	W	Cricklewood
HD	Harrow Weald	WA*	Watford High Street
HE*	High Wycombe	WD	Wandsworth
HF*	Hatfield	WG	West Green
HG*	Hertford	WL	Walworth
HH*	Two Waters	WR*	Windsor
HN*	Hitchin	WY*	Addlestone
HW	Southall	X	Middle Row
J	Holloway	-	Aldenham (non-operational)

* indicates a Country Area garage.

As a result of service cuts implemented towards the end of November, coupled with earlier reductions to services introduced in August, three garages were made surplus to requirements and closed for operational purposes on the night of 25th/26th November. The three garages were:

CA   Clapham - later remembered for its use as the first part of the Museum of British Transport and many years later re-opened as a temporary operational garage while Norwood and later Streatham garages were being rebuilt. It was subsequently sold for re-development.

F   Putney Bridge - demolished within a few years and the site used for an office block.

P   Old Kent Road - site now developed as a Civic Centre but not before the building became a derelict hulk.

RT354 waits departure from Edgware Station on a short journey to Borehamwood although the via blind details the full service of Route 107 through to Ponders End. In the following year after overhaul the bus re-entered service at Turnham Green garage fitted with a non-roof box style body and continued in the ownership of London Transport until February 1976 when it was disposed of for scrap. (A.R. Packer)

APPENDIX II

A special thank-you is extended to the following correspondents for the interest shown in up-dating or correcting information given in earlier titles in this series of books and in certain cases providing valuable details for this volume. They are: Laurie Akehurst, Ken Archer, Eric Baker, John Bush, Colin Bull, Terry Dendy, Michael Dryhurst, John Gallard, G.P.Green, John Hillman, Ian MacDonald, Barry Maynard-Smith, John Nye, Chris Stewart, Dave Stewart, Reg Westgate and Alan Wood.

1939-1945 BOOK

Page 64   T596 in the upper picture stands beside The Crown public house in Little Missenden, whose landlord is Ron How, a well-known former Wimbledon Speedway rider.

Page 130   The vehicle in the upper picture is a Ford military 4x4 15cwt. truck and not a Chevrolet. Both this vehicle and the correctly captioned Chevrolet C15A in the lower picture on page 131 were built in Canada and shipped to the United Kingdom in knocked-down condition where they were assembled and wooden British built bodies added.

1947 BOOK

Page 89   The lower picture of ex-TD193 is taken at the Pier Head, Liverpool not St.Thomas Street as stated.

1955 BOOK

Page 120   In the lower picture RTL111 has just turned out of Colindale trolleybus depot, which is hidden by the bus. The car showrooms are still there today but under a different name.

1956 BOOK

Page 73   It has been pointed out that at this time Route 230 had two low bridges to contend with - the other being at Christchurch Avenue, Wealdstone where the Harrow - Stanmore branch line crossed.

Page 88   The Maidstone & District coach in the background is SKE995 with fleet number CO299, not CO229.

Page 134   The lower picture was taken inside Chiswick Works. Trolleybus traction poles and overhead wiring is just visible behind in Chiswick High Road.

1957 BOOK

Page 16   In the lower picture the previous owner of ex-STL1959 quoted as Hants & Dorset should read Hants & Sussex.

Page 18   The conversion of 2d. should be less than 1p and not 5p as given in the lower caption.

Page 29   The bottom picture of 408W shows it crossing Cricklewood Broadway into Cricklewood Lane, probably heading for either Golders Green or Cockfosters Underground Depot.

Page 53   The car beside the STL in the lower picture is not a Metropolitan but a larger U.S. built Nash.

Page 54   The location of the top picture is Ingrave Road, Brentwood and the ECW bodied Bristol bus in the background is working for Eastern National on a former City Coach Company route, having just turned from the High Street.

Page 58   The initials TMS on ex-D28 in the upper picture stand for Trimdon Motor Services, not Transport Motor Services.

Page 72   With reference to the lower caption, it has been pointed out that the 700 RF class vehicles were also fitted with quarter drop windows.

Page 77	In the lower caption British Airways Corporation should read British European Airways.
Page 84	The Leyland double deck in the background of the upper picture is a pre-war TD4 model, not a post-war PD1.
Page 99	The lower picture is of TD89, not TD69.
Page 125	The Morris Minor car is a Mark II, not a 1000 model.

1962 BOOK

Page 114	In the lower picture RLH70 is seen in Station Road, North Harrow near the junction with Pinner Road.
Page 144	RTL1630 in the top picture is at the Thornton Heath Clock Tower stand, not at Thornton Heath Pond which was not served by the 159.

Victoria Station forecourt on Monday 5th May, the first working day following the start of the all-out strike which lasted seven weeks. The bus lanes are deserted while the taxi rank does brisk business, even though the morning rush hour has passed. A clear and unobstructed view of the London Transport bus signs, based on the original LGOC 'tombstone' designed flags, stand like memorials to the absent buses. The base structure of the earlier gantry of the inspectors' departure control office stands to the extreme left of the picture. (N. Rayfield)

VEHICLE INDEX

Class	Number	Page	Class	Number	Page	Class	Number	Page	Class	Number	Page
4RF4	NLP639	13	RF	29	58	RT	76	78	RT	1199	24
4RF4	NLP640	13	RF	186	114	RT	84	78	RT	1204	22
B	19	115	RF	202	74	RT	152	119	RT	1214	27
C	65	143	RF	261	109	RT	154	57	RT	1224	52
CR	30	146	RF	369	107	RT	156	127	RT	1339	37
CR	33	146	RF	421	114	RT	166	42	RT	1348	26
CR	40	146	RF	430	55	RT	167	53	RT	1404	100
CRL	4	66	RF	440	14	RT	174	25	RT	1432	31
D	53	59	RF	454	118	RT	174	57	RT	1456	22
D	75	49	RF	492	112	RT	185	126	RT	1458	19
D	84	50	RF	508	36	RT	195	99	RT	1463	117
D	136	109	RF	514	87	RT	206	34	RT	1472	97
D	152	44	RF	528	105	RT	212	96	RT	1501	70
D	185	62	RF	535	19	RT	230	85	RT	1518	15
D	188	40	RF	558	121	RT	251	53	RT	1519	87
D	280	37	RF	585	47	RT	254	66	RT	1535	102
G	149	146	RF	599	119	RT	294	65	RT	1661	124
GS	4	88	RF	607	49	RT	327	69	RT	1668	85
GS	11	39	RF	608	58	RT	352	150	RT	1708	65
GS	14	62	RF	617	117	RT	354	156	RT	1763	101
GS	29	60	RF	620	50	RT	389	101	RT	1778	42
GS	34	35	RF	627	91	RT	423	95	RT	1816	15
GS	37	93	RF	632	69	RT	426	57	RT	1862	85
GS	38	27	RF	659	40	RT	430	106	RT	2026	58
GS	38	129	RF	679	77	RT	502	106	RT	2050	68
GS	44	94	RF	700	101	RT	571	70	RT	2122	60
GS	44	113	RFW	5	47	RT	573	45	RT	2339	97
GS	47	45	RFW	11	124	RT	656	91	RT	2365	36
GS	61	34	RLH	12	93	RT	758	38	RT	2370	115
GS	63	128	RLH	14	28	RT	760	39	RT	2410	24
GS	67	128	RLH	18	113	RT	911	35	RT	2443	39
GS	76	105	RLH	39	107	RT	912	120	RT	2468	7
LT	391	134	RLH	49	108	RT	951	74	RT	2521	26
LT	1015	135	RLH	71	48	RT	963	112	RT	2655	33
LT	1101	136	RM	1	54	RT	976	46	RT	2691	147
LT	1112	138	RM	2	63	RT	980	88	RT	2776	67
RF	10	71	RT	27	72	RT	1016	17	RT	3018	73
RF	18	125	RT	31	95	RT	1051	120	RT	3020	123
RF	21	76	RT	40	78	RT	1170	30	RT	3113	77

Class	Number	Page	Class	Number	Page	Class	Number	Page	Class	Number	Page
RT	3125	90	RTL	20	21	ST	1060	134	T	668	95
RT	3242	68	RTL	38	31	ST	1120	135	T	744	72
RT	3245	106	RTL	39	31	STD	23	147	T	786	102
RT	3269	46	RTL	41	18	STD	72	122	T	786	148
RT	3269	61	RTL	62	48	STD	72	122	T	792	71
RT	3314	106	RTL	85	51	STD	96	89	T	796	110
RT	3316	42	RTL	178	76	STD	105	139	TD	32	98
RT	3349	55	RTL	400	54	STD	130	153	TD	33	153
RT	3395	63	RTL	482	16	STL	441	147	TD	35	104
RT	3440	73	RTL	541	29	STL	670	154	TD	36	21
RT	3540	44	RTL	764	32	STL	971	78	TD	39	32
RT	3605	94	RTL	770	104	STL	980	133	TD	51	57
RT	3655	13	RTL	798	42	STL	1011	149	TD	58	89
RT	3708	92	RTL	824	96	STL	1026	140	TD	58	98
RT	3816	52	RTL	834	147	STL	1218	151	TD	81	138
RT	3868	59	RTL	847	147	STL	1428	148	TD	85	130
RT	3915	103	RTL	877	123	STL	1642	144	TD	91	17
RT	3995	126	RTL	1040	20	STL	1677	150	TD	95	64
RT	4192	94	RTL	1090	20	STL	1677	152	TD	101	86
RT	4277	78	RTL	1174	41	STL	1940	152	TD	112	89
RT	4344	28	RTL	1355	104	STL	2008	131	TD	122	25
RT	4407	13	RTL	1432	64	STL	2117	78	TD	128	23
RT	4448	12	RTL	1579	36	STL	2147	145	TF	23	145
RT	4554	35	RTL	1600	103	STL	2170	151	S/V	015GH	116
RT	4580	110	RTL	1620	33	STL	2194	56	S/V	38H	136
RT	4584	92	RTL	1621	125	STL	2348	152	S/V	725J	75
RT	4604	100	RTL	1630	111	STL	2595	29	ENOC	3905	142
RT	4605	90	RTW	3	79	STL	2656	141	NonLT	ABE335	84
RT	4610	38	RTW	85	86	T	250	140	NonLT	BFN934	83
RT	4614	16	RTW	119	129	T	251	137	NonLT	CRX540	82
RT	4625	67	RTW	247	139	T	261	149	NonLT	DBC224	80
RT	4697	26	RTW	289	108	T	276	149	NonLT	DUC904	83
RT	4699	51	RTW	324	116	T	416	43	NonLT	FT5702	80
RT	4714	96	RTW	417	121	T	424	146	NonLT	FTD612	83
RT	4727	75	SRT	50	139	T	454	144	NonLT	FTD618	82
RT	4746	14	ST	140	142	T	460	154	NonLT	GCD688	81
RT	4759	18	ST	249	131	T	466	143	NonLT	HTC615	84
RT	4762	118	ST	274	137	T	484	132	NonLT	JG9956	81
RTL	5	41	ST	314	143	T	555	133	NonLT	RPG491	127
RTL	9	56	ST	587	130	T	630	132	Victoria Station		158